A GREAT WEEKEND IN
LISBON

LISBON, THE DELIGHTFUL SHORE

Lisbon has been loved by all the people who have settled here over the years, as much for its temperate climate and pleasant way of life, as for its strategic location, which favours trade and commerce. Lisbon was first settled by the Phoenicians 3,000 years ago, who called it *Alis-Ubo*, meaning 'delightful shore'. Later the Romans renamed it *Olisipo*, believing the city to have been founded by Ulysses. Julius Caesar honoured it with the title *Felicitas Julia*, and the Moors cherished it as their *Aschbouna*.

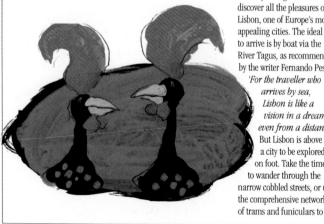

A weekend (even a long one) is barely enough time to discover all the pleasures of Lisbon, one of Europe's most appealing cities. The ideal way to arrive is by boat via the River Tagus, as recommended by the writer Fernando Pessoa:
'For the traveller who arrives by sea, Lisbon is like a vision in a dream, even from a distance.'
But Lisbon is above all a city to be explored on foot. Take the time to wander through the narrow cobbled streets, or use the comprehensive network of trams and funiculars to

climb the steeper hills, from where you'll discover panoramic views over the whole city. Take a peek at the traditional secret inner courtyards, admire the photogenic façades, decorated with colourful azulejo tiles, which are a notable feature of the city, and climb the impressive *escadinhas* (steps) to reach stunning *miradouros* (viewpoints). Make sure you occasionally glance down as under your feet the little black-and-white paving stones of the *calçada portuguesa* form a fascinating two-tone mosaic that glistens in the sunlight. Wander down the grand, palm-lined *avenidas*, the ideal place for window-shopping, and enjoy the majesty of the formally landscaped parks. The Portuguese are particularly proud of their terraces and gardens, and the scents of jasmine, geranium, lemon and jacaranda hang in the air, producing a wonderful heady fragrance. Another Portuguese passion is food. Lisbon has thousands of cafés and restaurants which offer tempting dishes at very reasonable prices. Stop off at one of the many patisseries to sample the *pasteis* (pastries)

and *bolos* (cakes), and make sure you try a *pasteis de nata* (custard-cream tart), which is a Portuguese speciality. Seafood is also widely available, and you mustn't leave without trying the *bacalhau* (salted cod), a delicious staple of Portuguese cuisine. Lastly, take advantage of your stay in the city to discover Portuguese wine, as well as other local specialities such as port and *ginginha* (cherry brandy). Lisbon also provides a wealth of opportunities for leisurely shopping. Handmade items are still the best buy when it comes to goods made in Portugal, and if you're keen on traditional crafts and have a nose for a bargain, you can find some wonderful gifts to take home. Don't be taken in by the city's sleepy atmosphere in the daytime, as it really comes alive at night. The narrow streets of the Bairro Alto and the banks of the River Tagus have become home to a buzzing nightlife. The old dockland districts, the

Docas, are now the favourite haunt of Lisbon's clubbers. Local architects have joined forces to turn the once seedy industrial landscape into a mecca for the young and trendy, and have created *the* place to be seen at the weekend. You, too, can join the throngs of pleasure-seekers in the *Docas* or Bairro Alto, let your hair down in a Cape Verde club,

or fall under the spell of the haunting melody of an authentic *fado*. Since ancient times no visitor has managed to resist Lisbon's charms, and you're bound to want to return to explore this magical city even further.

How to get there

Thanks to a temperate climate, Lisbon is hospitable all year round. Never too cold in winter or too hot in summer, the city is pleasant whatever the season. The proximity of the Atlantic Ocean can make the weather very changeable, but the sudden showers usually stop as quickly as they start.

THE BEST TIME TO GO

June and December are especially good months to visit the city. June is the ideal time to get to know the typical districts, especially during the Festas dos Santos Populares, when the streets are filled with jubilant crowds both day and night. December also offers a number of advantages. The city is festooned with Christmas decorations from the beginning of the month, and the shops, their window displays at their very best, are open at weekends. You can also sample some of the delicious Christmas pastries, such as *bolo rei,* a mouth-watering brioche with crystallised fruit. On the other hand, the Easter period (Good Friday is a holiday, Easter Monday is not) and 15 August (a public holiday) aren't good times to go unless you're seeking solitude. Everyone leaves for the Algarve and the shops are *fechado* (closed). With the city empty, it could be a little dreary.

AVERAGE TEMPERATURES

Jan. to Mar.:	17°C/63°F
Apr. to Jun.:	22°C/71°F
Jul. to Sep.:	26°C/79°F
Oct. to Dec.:	17°C/63°F

HOW TO GET THERE

The only realistic way you can get to Lisbon for a weekend is by plane (it would take over 20 hours by train from the UK).

BY PLANE FROM THE UK

British Airways
☎ 0345 222111
www.britishairways.com
Daily flights direct from Heathrow

Go
☎ 0845 6054321
www.gofly.com
Daily direct flights from London Stanstead.

TAP
☎ 0845 6010932
www.tap-airportugal.pt
Daily direct flights from
Heathrow.

FROM IRELAND
TAP
☎ 0845 6010932
www.tap-airportugal.pt
Direct scheduled flight from
Dublin every Saturday.

British Airways
☎ 0345 222111
www.britishairways.com
Flights to Lisbon via London.

FROM THE US
TAP, Delta (in a code-sharing
agreement with TAP), TWA
and Continental operate direct
scheduled flights from the US
to Lisbon.

Continental
☎ 1800 231 0856
www.continental.com
Daily flights from Newark.

Delta
☎ 1800 241 414
www.delta-air.com
New York to Lisbon, code-
sharing on a TAP flight, with
connections from many
major US cities.

TAP
☎ 1800 221 7370
www.tap-airportugal.pt
Daily flights from New York
or Newark.

TWA
☎ 1800 221 2000
www.twa.com
Daily flights from New York,
with connections from many
major US cities.

FROM CANADA
Air Canada
☎ 1800 776 3000
www.aircanada.ca
Flights from Toronto, Montreal
and Vancouver via London,
Frankfurt or Zurich with code
shares with European carriers.

Air France
☎ 1800 237 2747
www.airfrance.com
Flights from major Canadian
cities via Paris.

FROM AUSTRALIA
AND NEW ZEALAND
British Airways
Aus: ☎ 02 8904 8800
NZ: ☎ 09 356 8690

Flights from major cities
via London.

KLM
Aus: ☎ 03 9654 5222
NZ: ☎ 09 309 1782
Daily flights from Sydney to
Lisbon via Amsterdam

Qantas
Aus: ☎ 131 313
NZ: ☎ 09 357 8900
www.qantas.com
Daily flights from capital
cities with code-sharing
arrangements giving
connections to Lisbon.

INCLUSIVE
BREAKS

Many tour operators offer
two and three-day weekend
breaks that include travel by
plane and accommodation
in various categories of hotel,
as well as car hire if you want
to explore Sintra or the coast.
If you are travelling from the
UK the following companies
offer short breaks to Lisbon,
with prices starting at about
£250 for two nights:

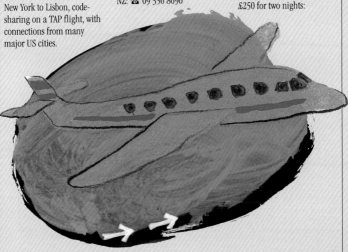

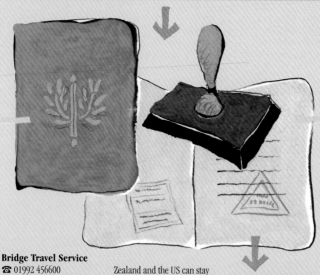

Bridge Travel Service
☎ 01992 456600

British Airways Holidays
0870 2424243

The Magic of Portugal
☎ 020 8741 1181

Sovereign
☎ 08702 430 635

Travelscene
☎ 020 8427 4445

ENTRY REQUIREMENTS

Nationals of all EU countries, as well as those from New Zealand and the US can stay up to three months without a visa. Australian citizens must obtain a visa from their nearest Portuguese consulate before entering the country. Visa requirements do change so it is advisable to check the current situation before travelling.

CUSTOMS

Portugal is part of the European Union and citizens of member states no longer have to pass through customs on arrival in the country. All you need is your passport. There's no limit on the amount or value of goods, including cigarettes and alcohol, you can buy for your personal use, and no customs formalities to complete on leaving Portugal. You can also bring whatever you like with you into the country, including your favourite foods. There are restrictions for non-EU citizens, however, (see page 87) and when entering the

country they must also declare money over 2,5000,000esc and pay tax on objects worth more than 35,000esc. For more information, contact your nearest international airport.

the traffic. The best way to get to the centre is by taxi, but only take an official taxi (black and green or beige) and make sure the driver starts the meter.

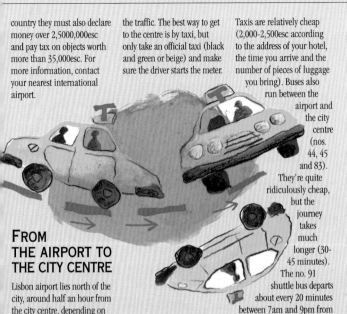

FROM THE AIRPORT TO THE CITY CENTRE

Lisbon airport lies north of the city, around half an hour from the city centre, depending on

Taxis are relatively cheap (2,000-2,500esc according to the address of your hotel, the time you arrive and the number of pieces of luggage you bring). Buses also run between the airport and the city centre (nos. 44, 45 and 83). They're quite ridiculously cheap, but the journey takes much longer (30-45 minutes). The no. 91 shuttle bus departs about every 20 minutes between 7am and 9pm from

---

PUBLIC HOLIDAYS AND SPECIAL EVENTS

Apart from the traditional holidays (25 December, 1 January, 1 May, 15 August and 1 November), there are many other holidays to take into account when planning a weekend in Lisbon. On these days, the banks, shops and most of the museums in the city are shut.

25 April (Liberty Day, celebrating the 1974 revolution): large-scale official commemorations and military parades in Lisbon.

June (Corpus Christi): falls on a different day in June each year. Religious processions.

10 June (anniversary of the death of Camões): Portugal Day, the national holiday.

5 October (Republic Day): official celebrations.

1 and 8 December (Independence Day, commemorating the restoration of independence from Spain in 1640, and the Feast of the Immaculate Conception): religious processions. To these must be added Good Friday and Shrove Tuesday, which fall on different dates according to the year.

On the other hand, the Festas dos Santos Populares in June (see page 29) are a

time of folk processions, street shows and fireworks, when the genuine popular enthusiasm is worth sharing. The events include:

12 June: a procession of the districts of Lisbon (*marchas populares*) in Avenida da Liberdade and a procession in the Alfama with the statue of St Antony.

12 to13 June: St Antony's Days (a holiday).

23 and 24 June: St John's Days.

28 and 29 June: St Peter's Days.

12 and 29 June: the festival of the sea at Cascais.

outside the terminal and runs to Praca do Marques de Pombal, Praca dos Restaurodores, Rossio, Praca do Comercio and Cais do Sodré train station.

CAR HIRE

All the major international car hire companies can be found in the airport (see page 33). If you want a child's seat or a special car, such as a people carrier, it's essential to book before leaving.

HEALTH

No vaccinations are needed before entering Portugal and the tap water is perfectly safe to drink. The products of the major pharmaceutical

USEFUL ADDRESSES

Portuguese Tourist Offices Abroad

US
590 Fifth Ave, 4th Floor
New York, NY 10036-4704
☎ 212 354 4403

Canada
500 Sherbrooke Street West,
Suite 940
Montreal QC H3A 3CS
☎ 514 282 1264

UK
22-25A Sackville Street, 2nd-4th floor London W1X 2LY
☎ 020 7494 1441

Ireland
54 Dawson Street, Dublin 2
☎ 670 9133

Australia/New Zealand
There are no Portuguese tourist offices in Aus or NZ but the following website has information on Lisbon:
www.consulportugalsydney.org.au

USEFUL WEBSITES
These websites are reliable and regularly updated:
www.eunet.pt
www.portugalvirtual.pt
www.portugalinsite.pt
www.atl-turismolisboa.pt

companies are available in Lisbon and you should be able to find most of your usual medicines, often with the same name as at home. However, if you're on a course

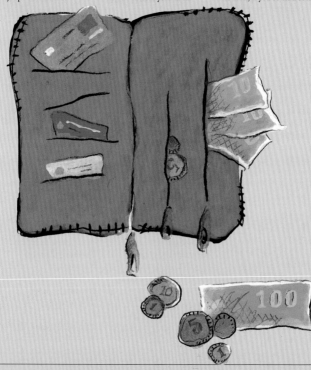

of medical treatment, it's best to take enough medicines with you. Citizens of European Union countries should obtain form E111 from their local post offices before departure and will then be entitled to free medical assistance, however, it is advisable to take out health insurance before travelling. In case of an emergency call:

☎ **115** (general emergency, fire, police, ambulance) or ☎ **112**

24-hr police:
☎ 213 466 141

The British Hospital:
☎ 213 955 067.

INSURANCE

UK tour operators are obliged by law to offer insurance, but it varies from company to company. You may find you are covered against theft, health problems and repatriation but not loss of luggage or cancellation. Before buying additional travel insurance, check your home, car and medical policies, as well as any cover provided by credit card companies, and always use a reputable, well-known insurer.

VOLTAGE

The electric current in Portugal is 220 volts, but you may need to use an adaptor.

LOCAL TIME

The time in Portugal is the same as Greenwich Mean Time. Summertime applies from the end of March, when clocks are put forward an hour, to the end of October, when they're put back an hour.

WHAT TO PACK

It's difficult to know what to pack for a weekend in Lisbon. You can get almost any kind of weather and forecasting is a hit and miss affair. On fine winter days, your warm coat will be quite superfluous, in summer, you may need something windproof to wear in the evening and whatever the season, an Atlantic cloud can bring a sudden shower. So here are a few suggestions:
• A raincoat with a quilted lining (between Nov. and Mar.), and a lighter windproof version (between Apr. and Oct.).
• A folding umbrella.
• A cardigan, pullover or sweatshirt (for summer evenings, or when you visit a museum or eat at a restaurant in winter – as some places have little or no heating).
• Comfortable shoes with non-slip soles (streets in the city centre are hilly and the paving stones can be slippery).
• Light clothes that you can layer in summer (the weather can be changeable over the course of a day).
• A swimming costume (if your hotel has a pool, or you fancy a dip in the Atlantic).

CURRENCY AND BUDGETING

Unless you opt for the Palace International and first-class restaurants, life is less expensive in Lisbon than in some other European cities. A meal in a medium-class restaurant (2 or 3 stars) will cost you 3,500-5,000esc per person. In a *tasca* or bistro, you're unlikely to spend more than 2,500esc. A bus ticket costs 80esc, a metro ticket 100esc, entrance to a museum 250-600esc, a concert seat 2,500-7,000esc, a *fado* show (including dinner) 4,500-8,000esc and entrance to a disco 8,000-10,000esc. Apart from air travel and hotel accommodation (which is difficult to estimate as it depends on the category), you can expect to pay 27,500-42,800esc for out-of-pocket expenses. As for souvenirs, you'll find plenty to tempt you if you like arts and crafts (azulejo tiles, wrought-iron items, household linen and embroidered tablecloths), leather goods at unbeatable prices or good wine (including port and madeira). Everything will seem relatively cheap, but it's a good idea to set 7,650-15,300esc aside for souvenirs.
The local currency is the escudo (esc), and there are currently around 315esc to the pound. Portugal is one of the European Union countries that joined the single currency, and the euro will replace the Escudo from 2002. In the meantime, prices are often listed in both escudos and euros. You can change some money before you go, but you'll find full money-changing facilities at Lisbon airport, including automatic money-changing and cash machines. You can also withdraw escudos in machines everywhere using your credit card.

THE GOLDEN AGE AND THE GREAT DISCOVERIES

The 15th-century expeditions to the New World marked the start of a period of prosperity for Lisbon as it prepared to take on a new role at the centre of world trade.

Vasco da Gama

PRINCE HENRY THE NAVIGATOR, AN EFFECTIVE SPONSOR

Prince Henry the Navigator, known as the father of the discoveries, used his own fortune and the wealth of the Order of Christ (of which he was the governor), to finance naval expeditions. As the uncle and adviser of King Afonso V (1438–1481), he founded the first Portuguese school of navigation and persuaded the nobility to invest in the emerging ship-building industry. He helped to design caravelles, the fast Portuguese ships, and improved the techniques of navigation and cartography, but never actually left dry land himself.

THE DISCOVERY OF THE WORLD

Despite being situated on the edge of Europe, Lisbon rapidly became the centre of a vast global empire due to its naval discoveries. After the colonisation of Madeira and the Azores, and the subsequent expeditions to explore the coast of Africa, Bartolomeu Dias rounded the Cape of Good Hope in 1487, paving the way for Vasco da Gama's voyage to India in 1498–99. In 1500, following a navigational error, Pedro Alvares Cabral discovered Brazil while in command of a fleet of twelve ships bound for India. Some twenty years later, the Portuguese explorer Fernão de Magalhães (Ferdinand Magellan), sailing on behalf of King Charles V of Spain, undertook the first circumnavigation of the globe, establishing beyond any possible doubt that the Earth was round.

A TIME OF PROSPERITY

Lisbon boomed with the influx of goods brought by the development of trade in sugar, dyes, spices and precious woods, and a new gold-based currency, the cruzado, was issued. As the city expanded, the banks of the Tagus were filled in to accommodate customs houses, warehouses and an arsenal. Lisbon became the centre for cartography and the manufacture of maritime instruments and an amazing number of palaces, hospitals and 4- and 5-storey houses were erected, the rich merchants living on the top floors, with the best-stocked shops in Europe beneath.

THE MANUELINE STYLE, THE LEGACY OF EXPLORATION

The routes to India and Brazil were opened up in the reign of Manuel I (1495–1521), whose government attracted talented people from across Europe and who encouraged all the arts – painting, illumination, gold- and silversmithing and sculpture. The Manueline style is characterised by maritime symbols, including the armillary sphere and cross of the Order of Christ, anchors, ropes, shells and exotic marine plants and animals.

CAMÕES, THE POET OF THE GOLDEN AGE

In *Os Luciados*, the epic poem about the discoveries, Camões traces Vasco da Gama's journey to India and describes his extraordinary adventures.

'With the pilots on the sandy beach
To find out where we were,
I set about
Measuring the height of the sun and measuring the distance
With a compass on the map of the world.'

Luis Vaz de Camões, *Os Luciados*.

The extraordinary architecture is best seen in places such as the Mosteiro dos Jéronimos (see page 46).

RIVALRY WITH SPAIN

Portugal rivalled Spain in the race for new lands, and the zones of influence of the two nations were very soon defined. In 1494, with the Pope as arbitrator, the Treaty of Tordesillas was signed, giving all the land lying east of a line 370 leagues from the Cape Verde islands to Portugal,

including Africa, the Orient, and Brazil (which was yet to be discovered). Beyond this 370 league limit, all new territories would be subject to Spanish sovereignty.

THE INEVITABLE DECLINE

Even though Portugal was the centre of the most far-flung trading empire in the world, cracks soon began to appear in its organisation. The local population became unable to supply the governors, soldiers, sailors and colonists who were required to administer and control the conquered lands, and at the end of the 16th century the failure of the *Casa das Indias* (the national trading company) and King

UNUSUAL SOUVENIRS

For reproductions of items that summon up the age of exploration – astrolabes, model ships, East India Company china etc try: **Sociedade Historica da Independência de Portugal, Rua das Portas de S. Antão, 2-A, ☎ 21 342 89 87, Mon.-Sat. 11.30am-7.30pm.**
For 16th-, 17th- and 18th-century nautical maps, books and rare objects:
Pesquisa Historica de Rainer Daehnardt, Centro Comercial Amoreiras, Loja 1031/1027 ☎ 21 383 32 49, Mon.-Sun. 10am-11pm.

Sebastian's disastrous crusade against the Moors, marked the end of the empire. Spain seized the opportunity to annex her rival and dominated Portugal for the next 80 years.

VIEWPOINTS AND FUNICULARS: A BIRD'S-EYE VIEW OF LISBON

Finding your way round Lisbon can be quite a challenge. Fortunately, there's a comprehensive network of trams following picturesque routes, and funiculars which climb seemingly impossible gradients.

THE CITY OF THE SEVEN HILLS

'The vast, irregular, multi-coloured mass of houses that make up Lisbon are scattered over seven hills. These are marvellous places from which to see the magnificent views. For the traveller who arrives by sea, Lisbon appears like a vision in a dream. Even from a distance, it stands out clearly against the bright blue of a sky that is heated by the gold of the sun. The domes, the monuments and the castles rise above the jumble of houses.'
Fernando Pessoa, *Lisbon*.

TRAMS

On 31 August 1901, a new, electrically-powered public transport system was inaugurated. At 6 o'clock in the morning, the first *eléctrico* (tram) in Lisbon, newly arrived from the factories of Philadelphia, began its run on the Cais do Sodré-Algès line, and the *eléctricos* have been climbing the steep city streets ever since. They've changed little over the years, except for being plastered with more and more advertisements, and the driver still gets off to change the switches by hand. One of the best ways to discover the city is to rattle along on a no. 25 or 28 tram, which pass along some of Lisbon's most picturesque streets. If you want to be sure of getting a seat, go to the terminus (the Dos Prazeres cemetery for the no. 28 and Praça da Estrela for the no. 25) but avoid the rush hours at all costs (8.30-9.30am, 4.30-6.30pm).

INDISPENSABLE FUNICULARS

Lisbon has a good public transport system, which is fortunate as some of the flights of steps, such as the *caracol* leading to the *miradouro* de Graça, seem to go up and up for ever. The cobbled streets are also a nightmare if you're wearing high-heeled shoes. With some of the steepest streets in Europe, it would be nearly impossible to get around Lisbon without the funiculars that ferry you from hill to hill.

A CHOICE OF FUNICULARS

The extremely useful **da Gloria funicular**, which runs both day and night, is difficult to miss and will take you from the Avenida de la Liberdade to the Bairro Alto, a stone's throw from the *miradouro* of São Pedro de Alcântara.

Some places particularly lend themselves to the melancholic musical strains of *saudade* (see p. 21). These include the Graça, Nossa Senhora do Monte, Santa Luzia, Castelo, S. Pedro de Alcântara and Santa Caterina *miradouros* and the Museu Nacional de Arte Antiga, not to mention all the stunning views from staircases, churches and porches that you'll discover by chance as you wander through the city.

The magical **da Lavra** funicular runs in practically the opposite direction to the da Gloria. From Rua das Portas de São Antão, it climbs ever upwards to reveal the most amazing views, but because of the steep descent, it's best to either buy a return ticket or wear shoes with non-slip soles. The **da Bica** funicular is the most overlooked. Hidden away in the shadow of one of the dark porches of Rua da Boa Vista, it takes you from Cais do Sodré to the heart of the picturesque Santa Caterina district, not far from the *miradouro* of the same name.

A CITY OF *MIRADOUROS*

Lisbon is the city of *miradouros* (viewpoints). Social places in the city, where friends meet to play cards, children come to ride their bicycles and lovers gaze out over the horizon, hand in hand. With superb views of the city at your feet and the River Tagus in the distance, on a clear day you can even just make out the Atlantic Ocean on the horizon.

THE *ELÉCTRICO DE TURISMO*

Carris, which operates Lisbon's public transport system, offers guided tours of the city in a charming red and gold tram – the *eléctrico de turismo*. The price of the tours is quite high when you consider that it's possible to follow almost the same route on one of the scheduled trams (nos. 28, 25 or 15), although you do get an English commentary and more comfortable seats on the tourist tram.

Eléctrico de Turismo, Carris, Praça do Comércio ☎ 21 363 93 43 Departures every day, 1.30pm and 3.30pm. Price 2,800esc (adults), 1,500esc (children).

AZULEJOS

Until the 16th century earthenware tiles weren't made in Portugal, but were imported from Spain where they were produced by Moorish craftsmen. However, when Italian artists settled in Lisbon in around 1550, they combined the fashionable tile support with an enamelled earthenware technique, and the Portuguese azulejo was born.

AN OMNIPRESENT DECORATIVE ART

In 1580 Portugal was a dependency of Spain, and the court and its retinue of artists resided in Madrid. Funds were lacking in Portugal, and as azulejo tiles were inexpensive

and easy to maintain, they replaced the paintings, carpets, sculptures and bas reliefs that people could no longer afford. They became so popular that the terraces, gardens and façades of churches, hospitals, palaces and villas were covered with them. They're still used today throughout Lisbon to decorate both private and public buildings.

THE ORIGIN OF THE NAME

Azulejos (pronounced 'azoolayjoush'), originally came from the Persian word

'Az-zulaÿ', meaning 'polished stone'. There are a number of different types of design:
Figura avulsa is an isolated, often simple design, usually done by an apprentice.
Padrão is a design spread over a number of tiles (4, 16 or 32) and is repeated indefinitely.
Painel (plural *painéis*) is like a panel, where a number of tiles are painted together to form a picture.
Registros are panels depicting the saints and are used over porches.

MAKING AZULEJO TILES

A square clay base is fired at 850–1,000°C/1,560–1,830°F, then covered in raw glaze. The design is traced in graphite and then painted with metal oxides using a special brush, taking care that the hands never touch the design. Before firing, the blues (cobalt) often look mauve, and the greens (copper) look greyish – only the yellows (antimony) and browns

COLOURS AND DESIGNS THROUGH THE CENTURIES

16th and early 17th century: multi-coloured figurative designs.
17th century: blue and yellow geometrical designs, and repetition of a *padrão*.
Late 17th and mid-18th century: blue and white *figura avulsa* (flowers, birds, etc.) and *painéis* (court and hunting scenes, parties and the lives of saints).
Mid-18th century and 19th century: multi-coloured *registros* and *painéis* (scenes of everyday life and trade).
20th century: multi-coloured contemporary and abstract designs.

(manganese) are recognisable. The panels are painted on large easels, before being

taken apart, numbered and arranged square by square on trays inside the kiln. Azulejos are always fired at high temperatures (980–1,020°C/ 1,800–1,870°F).

RECOGNISING AZULEJO TILES
The quality of an azulejo (and therefore its price) depends on both the base tile

and the decorative design. Factory-made bases are moulded, cut and enamelled by machine, while handmade or semi-handmade bases are produced either wholly or partially by hand. In general, factory-made tiles are printed automatically (when producing large tiled surfaces), or stencilled (in the case of friezes), but can also be hand-painted (when creating decorative objects). Handmade and semi-handmade tiles are always hand-painted, and therefore each is unique. The difference between factory-made and handmade tiles is clear to the eye. If you examine the

designs and the colours closely a hand-painted tile will never be perfect, but that is its charm. Handmade and semi-handmade tiles have an irregular pinkish or yellow background, an embossed appearance, and are 7–9mm/0·28–0·35in thick, whereas factory-made tiles have a regular white or cream background and are 5–6mm/0·2–0·24in thick.

HOW TO USE AZULEJOS
Although azulejos were traditionally used to tile the walls and floors of bathrooms and kitchens, they're also now to be found in other rooms in the house in the form of tables, pictures and other decorative objects. The standard dimensions are 14x14cm or 15x15cm (5¹/₂x5¹/₂in or 6x6in) for walls and floors, and 7·5x5cm or 5x5cm (3x2in or 2x2in) for friezes. They can be

A SHOP TO REMEMBER
The renowned antique dealer, **Solar**, has a unique display of 16th-, 17th- and 18th-century azulejo tiles, including *figura avulsa* (5,000esc each), blue and yellow friezes (8,000esc each) and *painéis* of all sizes (up to 600,000esc for a 17th-century mounted panel 1x1.5m/ 39x 59in). Even if you aren't planning to buy, the shop is worth a look.
Solar, Rua Dom Pedro V, 68-70
☎ 21 346 55 22.
Mon.-Fri. 10am-7pm.

displayed on supports made of varnished or painted wood, cork (trays, table mats, etc.), on wrought-iron (tables), or on an acrylic base (8mm/0·3in thick), which can be hung on a wall. Cement glue is used to fix them onto walls and floors, silicon glue is used for acrylic supports and wood glue for wooden frames and objects.

PALACES AND GARDENS, A WHOLE WAY OF LIFE

In Lisbon you will find a wonderful array of gardens, ranging from simple balconies and tiny courtyards to magnificent parks lined with azulejos. As you walk about the city you will discover enchanting secret gardens, as well as a few *quintas* (grand country houses) and magnificent palaces.

SECRET GARDENS

If you stroll around Lisbon in the spring, you'll get the impression of being in the countryside. Your senses will be overwhelmed by the perfume of jasmine and orange blossom and the rich colours of the jacarandas, bougainvillaeas and geraniums are a delight to the eye. There are little gardens everywhere in Lisbon. All you have to do is find them – sometimes hidden behind high walls in Lapa, covered in weeds in the heart of the Bairro Alto, or tucked away in the corner of a balcony in the Alfama. Nettles and wild cabbage sometimes even grow between the paving stones.

RETIROS...

Lisbon was once surrounded by *retiros* and *quintas*.

These two words have no direct translations and they reflect a typically Portuguese lifestyle. *Retiros* were fine houses built close to the city, yet at the same time far enough away to ensure a peaceful and quiet life. People would 'retire' to them to enjoy themselves in private, or to carry on secret affairs. Unfortunately, most of these properties have now been swallowed up by the city and have vanished without trace. Only one, the Palácio Pimenta, has been preserved and it has been turned into a museum.

... AND *QUINTAS*

Quintas are large private country houses set in vast

stretches of farmland where noble families would spend the summer away from the heat of the city. They boast landscaped gardens as well as arable land, and are often more like small palaces than farms. The area around

Lisbon is filled with these charming properties, and fortunately some of them have been turned into guest houses which often host music festivals in the summer (especially in the area around Sintra). Others, such as the Palácio Fronteira, which boasts beautiful gardens filled with wonderful statues and fountains, have become museums.

QUINTA DOS MARQUÊS DA FRONTEIRA
☎ 21 778 45 99
Every day except Sun. and holidays, guided tour at 11am
Entry charge.

Situated in the Parque Florestal de Monsanto, this is one of the finest Portuguese *quintas*, and is easy to visit during a short stay in Lisbon. The park is a delightful place for a walk, thanks to an outstanding collection of azulejos. Take a stroll through the Gallery of Kings, the *casa do fresco* and the grand terrace, as well as the interior of the palace, with its magnificent Victory Room lined with azulejos illustrating Portugal's great victories against Spain. The *quinta* is still inhabited by the descendants of its founder, so the number and times of tours can vary. It's best to telephone in advance to find out exactly what's open to visitors (gardens, palace or both) and what time you can visit.

PALÁCIO PIMENTA
Museu da Cidade
Campo Grande, 245
☎ 21 759 16 17

Tue.-Sun. 10am-1pm, 2-5pm
Entry charge.

This magnificent 18th-century palace was once a royal *retiro*, and still retains its magnificent gardens despite the encroachment of the

modern city. Unfortunately, these gardens, with their magnificent peacocks, are not open to the public and can only be seen from the gate. In the palace you should make sure you see the kitchen and staircases, which are entirely covered in blue and white azulejos, the 18th-century decor (furniture, objects and tableware), as well as the impressive dining room. Offering an interesting historical retrospective of Lisbon, the various stages in the life of the city can be pieced together from the remains on show, especially the Roman period, when Praça da Figueira was a necropolis and Lisbon was given the title *Felicita Julia* by Julius Caesar. Everything is remarkably well illustrated, and a huge model of the city is evidence of its great prosperity before the 1755 earthquake.

HANDMADE CRAFTS

Portugal has a rich and flourishing tradition of specialist handmade arts and crafts, including ceramics, embroidery and leatherwork. The regions' crafts are among the richest in Europe, and are some of the few to have retained their originality and traditions.

CERAMICS AND TABLEWARE

Several regions produce ceramics and tableware, all of which have very different characteristics.

Alcobaça tableware

With its floral or abstract motifs and colours (primarily greens, blues and yellows), this is probably the most modern tableware on offer today, as well as the most affordable (around 1,000esc a plate).

Caldas das Rainha ceramics

These owe their fame to Rafael Bordalo Pinheiro, whose originality was rewarded with a gold medal at the Universal Exhibition of 1889 in Paris. Baroque in style, some would say positively kitsch, they feature grotesque characters and objects, with fruit and flowers in relief.

Coimbra earthenware

This is one of the oldest centres of ceramic production in Portugal. It's very traditional in style and fairly expensive.

Alentéjo ceramics

These usually feature blue, green or multi-coloured floral patterns on a terracotta-coloured background, and include ovenproof tableware and dishes (Viana do Alentéjo), and decorative objects (Estremoz figurines).

Barcelos roosters

The emblem of Portugal, the rooster, is produced in bright colours on a black background. Made into items such as key-rings or corkscrews, it's an essential souvenir that won't break the bank.

A STITCH IN TIME

The timeless Madeira *bordados* (embroidery) is a good buy, and can sometimes even be an investment. The art of embroidery developed in Madeira in the late 19th century due to the efforts of an Englishwoman, and it quickly became a flourishing industry known throughout Europe. Linen, silk, cotton and organdie are still the main fabrics used, and the stitches vary according to the fabric and design. Madeira embroidery is a complex art made up of a large number of small stitches – *caseados* for the outlines, *Richelieu* or *bastidos* for the reliefs, and *estrelas, ilhas* and *folhas* for the designs.

The embroiderers still work from home for the manufacturers, who supply them with fabric on which the design has already been stencilled. Once finished, a piece is washed, ironed and submitted to the Madeira Craft Institute, where it is checked and a lead seal and certificate of guarantee is attached. This is vital proof of the authenticity of the piece, and also explains its high price (3,000–12,000esc for a place mat depending on size).

FESTIVE WHITE

In the north, in Viana do Castelo, the rich embroidery of the traditional Portuguese costumes has been transferred to tablecloths and napkins. Using floral or geometric designs, the embroidery is done in white thread on coloured cotton (bright blue,

green or red), or in yellow or blue thread on white or ecru cotton (expect to pay 15,000esc for a 1m20x1m20/48x48in tablecloth and six napkins). The most renowned *turcos* (terry-towelling) in the country is made in Torres Novas (less than 100km/60 miles from Lisbon). The towels bearing the Companhia de Torres Novas label are very soft and thick and are always made to the highest quality. A man's bathrobe costs around 6,500esc, and a set of five towels (1 bath towel, 2 hand towels and 2 guest towels) costs around 7–8,000esc.

USEFUL ADDRESSES

Regional ceramics and crafts
Santos Oficios
R. Madalena, 87 (Castelo)
☎ 21 887 20 31.
Mercearia Liberdade
Av. da Liberdade, 207
☎ 21 354 70 46.
Alcobaça tableware
Pollux
Rua dos Franqueiros, 276,
☎ 21 886 97 44.
A Zé
Rua das Padarias, 13 (Sintra).
the markets of Carcavelos
and **S. Pedro de Sintra**
(see page 67).
Madeira embroidery
Madeira House
Rua Augusta, 131-135
☎ 21 342 68 13.
Towels
O Bragal
Centro Comercial
Ibersil, Loja 46,
Av. da Liberdade, 38
☎ 21 342 51 78.
Turcos and
Bordados
Rua Ferreira Borges, 149 A,
☎ 21 385 24 50
(see page 103).

HOW TO TELL CERAMICS, EARTHENWARE AND PORCELAIN APART

Cerâmica (ceramics or pottery) is made from a clay and water-based paste, which is hand-painted and fired at 900–1,000°C/ 1,650–1,830°F to produce relatively thick, robust objects.

Faiança (earthenware) is made from a porous clay paste fired at around 920°C/1,690°F, then enamelled and painted. It's re-fired at 1,020°C/1,870°F for everyday objects or 1,400°C/ 2,550°F for fragile objects.

Grês (stoneware) is made from a silica-based paste, which is sometimes salted to make it stronger. It is painted and then fired at 1,280–1,300°C/ 2,340–2,370°F to make non-porous objects for cooking.

Porcelana (porcelain) is made from a mixture of kaolin, quartz and feldspar. It is fired twice at a high temperature before decoration, then a third time to make strong, delicate tableware.

FADO, THE SONG OF PORTUGAL

You may have heard of *fado*, the sad, langorous lament that expresses all the *saudade* and nostalgia of the Portuguese soul. As Lisbon is probably the best place to hear it, you should really try to fit in a *fado* evening, which will undoubtedly turn out to be a fascinating and moving experience.

AFRICAN ORIGINS

Opinions vary as to the origins of *fado*. Some believe they lie in the chants of sailors voicing their longing for home after months away at sea. Others suggest the melodies of Brazil or Africa as a starting point. Wherever it originated, *fado* appeared in Lisbon in the 18th century as a sensual dance based on African belly dancing. It slowly evolved into a plaintive melody, accompanied by musical arrangements on the guitar, and nowadays similar sounds can be heard in the Cape Verde *morna* sung by Cesaria Evora.

THE POPULAR SONG OF LISBON

For the people of Lisbon, the only 'true' *fado* is the kind you hear in Lisbon itself. For them, it's a street art that has nothing in common with the distinctive *fado* of Coimbra, which is intellectual, politically committed and usually sung by students.

In Lisbon, *fado* is sung by the men and women of the working-class districts, who gather in the taverns to express the beauty of their city, the pain of love and poverty, or the trials of being exiled far from their country.

A MELODRAMATIC SETTING

Fadistos (male singers) or *fadistas* (female singers) appear on stage dressed entirely in black. They stand straight-backed among the musicians, with their heads held high and a distant look in their eyes, and are then ready to begin. The two *guitarras*, typically Portuguese twelve-stringed instruments, produce slightly metallic sounds that accompany the whole melody like deep sobbing. Fortunately, the *violas* (Spanish guitars) add a lighter note.

CHIC *FADO*...

If you opt for typical restaurant *fado*, which is the chic version, you'll dine in soft lighting accompanied by the sounds of a variety of artists.

Such places can often be expensive and filled with tourists, so you need to choose carefully to be sure to get a good deal for your money. If you want to enjoy a high-quality show with professional, or even famous, singers and good cuisine, try **Sr Vinho** in the Lapa district. This nightclub belongs to the famous *fadista* Maria da Fé, who sings at the end of the evening. Another good place to try is **La Parreirinha** in the Alfama, where Maria's equally famous rival,

Argentina Santos, performs (see page 126 for addresses).

...OR STREET *FADO*

If you don't fancy going to a professional show you can hear authentic (but amateur) *fado vadio* in the Bairro Alto or the Alfama. You'll need to find a *tasca* (bistro) – often a tiny nightclub that doesn't look much on the outside, but where local people who are true amateurs come to sing after 11pm. Although you probably won't be able to sit comfortably and will have to wait to be served, it's here you'll hear authentic street *fado*. You can appreciate the true value of these sad melodies the local way, standing with a glass of *aguardente velha* (old brandy) in your hand.

SAUDADE AND SEBASTIANISM

The word *fado* comes from the Latin word *fatum*, meaning fate, and expresses a feeling similar to the blues, *saudade,* nostalgia for a happier past and helplessness in the face of passing time. But it also reflects the hope of Sebastianism – a strange belief which derives from an old legend. According to this story, the young king Sebastian did not die in the disastrous crusade against the Arabs in 1578 as is thought, but will one day return to save his country and restore its past glory.

The recordings of the legendary **Amália Rodrigues**, the grand old lady of *fado*, are always a good buy. Among the more contemporary classics, **Maria da Fé** and **Argentina Santos** are a safe bet. If you want to discover the younger generation that's been inspired by *fado* airs and modernised them, you'll be spoilt for choice. **Madredeus** is the group of Teresa Salgado, famous for the music of the Wim Wenders film, *Lisbon Story*. **V Imperio** is the rising star who's currently replacing Madredeus in the hearts of the local critics (*Mar de folhas*). Then there are the magical voices of **Dulce Pontes** (*Caminbos, Lagrimas,* etc.), **Misia** (*Tanto menos tanto mais*), **Amélia Muge** (*Todos os dias*) and **Paulo Brangança**, the most unusual of the contemporary *fadistos*. There's even a *fado* museum: **Casa do Fado and da Guitarra Portuguesa**, Largo do Chafariz do Dentro (see page 45).

TASTY LOCAL PRODUCE

Portuguese cuisine is rustic, country cooking that uses simple, local produce. Before you leave Lisbon, why not buy some authentic Alentéjo charcuterie, *queijo da Serra* and olive oil, not to mention a few pieces of the national delicacy *bacalhau* (dried cod)?

BACALHAU, THE MYTH AND THE LEGEND

Affectionately known as the *fiel amigo* (faithful friend), *bacalhau* (salted cod) is the national dish of Portugal, and there are said to be over 365 different ways of cooking it.

Dried cod has been eaten here for thousands of years, and Lisbon was famous in Roman times for exporting salted cod all over the empire. Nowadays, the cod is imported from Iceland or Norway, but as the North Sea fishing banks face extinction, it's best to try *bacalhau* while you still can.

HOW TO BUY *BACALHAU*

Bacalhau is dried and sold whole, including its skin and bones. You can choose your piece of fish, which will be cut up in front of you with a saw, and you can ask for the number of pieces (*a postas*) you want. One piece normally serves two people. The price per kg/2·2lb varies according to the size of the fish, as the thicker (and more expensive) it is, the more flesh it will have and the tastier it will be. Whether you want to buy some or not, take a wander down Rua do Arsenal (Baixa), where you'll find one traditional grocer's shop after another, all selling dried cod of varying quality.

EXTRA VIRGIN OLIVE OIL

Portugal is one of the three major olive oil producers of Europe, along with Spain and Italy, and the olives produced are highly flavoured, with a fruity and slightly bitter taste. The olives come mainly from Alentéjo, where they're harvested by hand or beaten down from the trees with long poles so that they fall into nets without being

damaged. You need 4–5kg/ 9–11lb of olives to make a litre of oil, and the yield per person is only 8–10kg/ 18–22lb an hour. The oil is made using a process that hasn't changed for centuries: the skin is removed, the olives are pressed, and the stones are crushed to separate the oil from the water and residues contained in the olives. This process and the origin of the olives determines the quality of the oil. It's best to choose an extra virgin oil (obtained by cold-pressing the olives) rather than a refined oil (obtained by heating), and select one with the lowest possible acidity rating (0·5° or 0·7°).

PORTUGUESE QUEIJO, THE GREAT UNKNOWN

Portugal produces vast quantities of *queijo* (cheese). Each *quinta* (agricultural estate) makes its own cheeses and it can be difficult to tell the various kinds apart as little attention is paid to marketing techniques – the cheeses are rarely branded and all have practically the same packaging. Make sure you try the *queijo de cabra* (goat's cheese) of Serpa or Castelo Branco, the creamy *queijo d'Azeitão* and, above all, the *queijo da Serra amanteigado*. To enjoy this properly, you should cut out the centre of this ripe ewe's *(ovelha)* cheese and eat it with a teaspoon. A good place to buy some is **Serra da Estrela**, Centro Comercial das Amoreiras (Av. Eng. Duarte Pacheco, Loja 3021-3056, open every day 10am-midnight ☎ 21 383 16 31).

COUNTRY FLAVOURS

Sausages and hams are the other local specialities that you really shouldn't miss. Several regions, including Beiras and Alentéjo, produce distinctive and flavoursome charcuterie with plenty of character. Although it may be a little heavy to transport, it is much cheaper than at home so you won't regret buying it in Portugal. If you're wondering what to get, you could try *presunto pata negra* (raw ham made from the black pigs of the north-east of the country), *chouriço* or *linguiça*, *farinheiras* or *alheiras* (traditional sausages that

you grill and eat hot) or *paios* (smoked sausages), which are a delicacy from Alentéjo.

A NEW CITY FOR THE ENLIGHTENMENT

On All Saints' Day in 1755, Lisbon was rocked by a violent and destructive earthquake. Afterwards, the Prime Minister of the time, Sebastião José de Carvalho, Marquês de Pombal, became the promoter of an urban and economic revolution. Inspired by the aestheticism and rationalism of the Enlightenment, he ordered the centre of Lisbon be razed to the ground to allow a new city to be built.

The Marquês de Pombal

THE GREAT EARTHQUAKE

On November 1, 1755, the first tremors were felt while the population celebrated mass, causing the vaults of several churches to collapse. As people panicked they headed for the river, but were forced back by a vast tidal wave. Lisbon had a large population for the time (250,000 people), and around 40,000 people died in the disaster and the famine and epidemics that followed.

Ruins of Lisbon as appeared immediately after the EARTHQUAKE and FIRE of the 1st of Nov. 1755.

THE TRIUMPH OF THE ENLIGHTENMENT

Pombal was given carte blanche by King José I to rebuild the city and to pursue his own political aims. As an enlightened and liberal minister, he initiated reforms in commerce, education, justice and the economy, and also abolished slavery. He was resolutely anti-clerical and his ambition was to transform the country by favouring the development of the middle classes at the expense of the nobility and clergy, who he felt were too powerful. He embarked upon a fierce crusade against the Jesuits, the dominant religious force in Portugal at the time.

A RATIONAL AESTHETIC

Pombal set out to modernize all aspects of the city after the great disaster. He adopted a functional approach to town planning and wanted to rationalise Lisbon as he rebuilt it in order to turn it into a model city. Winding streets and elaborate façades would be a thing of the past – the main roads would be straight and wide and the buildings would all look

exactly the same. For the first time, standardised materials would be used for all the building works, and these were often imported from across Europe. In concern for public health, Pombal also included wells, sewers, pavements and street paving in his plans.

THE BAIXA AND THE PROMOTION OF TRADE

Pombal's philosophy is apparent in the organisation of the Lower City (the Baixa). This was reserved for commerce and trade, and the shops were grouped by corporation. A class of merchants and bankers emerged, laying the foundations for the country's development by supporting its political activity and financing public works.

THE INVENTION OF FACTORY-MADE AZULEJOS

The traditional techniques used to decorate earthenware tiles were time-consuming and elaborate, and they failed to meet the need to produce tiles quickly. In 1767, the foundation of the royal earthenware factory in Rato made it possible to produce

tiles with simplified designs (garlands, shells, etc.) on a large scale. The tiles were based on a repetitive pattern and were used in corridors, staircases and kitchens. Multi-coloured designs were back in fashion and manganese gave the tiles a purplish-blue tinge typical of the period.

A FEEL FOR LEATHER

The tradition of leatherworking goes back a long way in Portugal. In the 14th century there were already tanners' workshops in the Alfama, where the natural springs favoured the washing and tanning of leather. Nowadays, Portugal is the second largest European producer of leather and shoes.

THE SECOND LARGEST EXPORTER OF SHOES IN EUROPE

Portugal produces 110 million pairs of shoes a year, of which 88 million are exported. This amounts to 8% of the country's total exports. Portugal is the second largest producer of shoes in Europe and the ninth largest in the world. Over 1,000 companies employ 50,000 people, with a total annual turnover of 350 billion escudos. These figures reveal the importance of shoe production to the country's economy.

FINE LEATHER FROM THE NORTH

Over 90%

of the leather and finished leather goods produced in Portugal come from the north of the country, but Portugal isn't totally self-sufficient in hides and some have to be imported. The Porto region specialises in the manufacture of expensive, high-quality shoes for men, women and children, and the little town of S. João de Madeira is famous throughout Portugal for its large number of factories. Middle-of-the-range footwear, mainly for men, is produced around Braga, while the manufacture of everyday shoes with leather uppers and rubber soles is concentrated in Leira, which is closer to Lisbon. There are still a few workshops producing women's luxury shoes in Lisbon itself.

JACKETS AND BAGS

Portugal produces a wide variety of leather goods, not only shoes, but also bags and clothes. Nowadays you will often find that the design is Italian but that the item has been manufactured in Portugal. This has created more fashionable items,

which are also reasonably priced so you can afford to buy a good pair of shoes or a leather jacket. Expect to pay 4,000–10,000esc for a good-quality handbag.

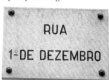

THE LEATHER STREET

Surprisingly, Rua 1° de Dezembro (Baixa), not Rua dos Sapateiros (Street of the Shoemakers), has the widest choice of leather shoes and accessories. There's an excellent selection of shops to choose from, and you'll find good-quality shoes in a range of mainly traditional styles. Expect to pay 12,000–15,000esc for a pair of men's shoes from S. João de Madeira. For women, the price range is wider depending on the style and colour (7,000–18,000esc).

DECIPHERING THE LABELS

Information about the shoe is written in Portuguese on the lining or may be illustrated with little drawings, or sometimes both together.

The following glossary will help you to understand what it all means.
Gàspea couro – leather upper.
Forro e palmilha em pele – leather interior and lining.
Sola couro – leather outer sole.
When buying clothes and accessories, always check that the label reading *couro verdadero* (real leather) is sewn inside.

FINDING SHOES THAT FIT

Portuguese shoes come in the usual continental sizes. However, sometimes the sizes are numbered from 1 to 6, in which case use the conversion chart below.
1 = 35/36 (UK 2/3)
2 = 37/38 (UK 4/5)
3 = 39/40 (UK 6/7)
4 = 41/42 (UK 8/9)
5 = 43/44 (UK 10/11)
6 = 45/46 (UK 12/13).
Shoe sizes can vary, so it's always safest to try them on before you buy them.

HAVING A SHOE-SHINE

If you want to make your shoes look like new again, take advantage of the last few wandering shoe shiners in the Baixa (on Praça do Rossio and Praça da Figueira). They're equipped with everything they need to do a very professional job, and as long as you

don't feel too ill at ease perched on a little stool having your shoes shone in public, you'll be delighted with the end result.

BOOTMAKERS TO THE RICH AND FAMOUS

Luis Barroso is one of the most celebrated bootmakers in the world, and his family has been making boots to measure for royalty and celebrities for two generations. For over ninety years, the choice of top-quality Portuguese leathers and traditional working methods have been a family secret. Only one hundred pairs of boots are made each year, including hunting boots, riding boots and ankle boots. All the boots are made by hand and are sold purely by word of mouth. Their most famous customers include not only the Spanish royal family, the Portuguese dukes of Bragança, ministers and members of parliament, but also Bo Derek and the daughter of Bing Crosby.
Sapataria Barroso,
Rua de Belém, 44
☎ 21 363 16 31,
Open weekdays 9am-1pm, 3-7pm.

SAINTS AND SOCCER

Portugal is the most devoutly Catholic country in Europe, and religious festivals are always fervently celebrated by the normally reserved inhabitants, turning areas of Lisbon into one big street party. Only football, Portugal's national game, and *touradas* (bullfighting) come close to arousing comparable enthusiasm.

A CHURCH WITH AN EVENTFUL PAST

The people of Portugal, the country of the Virgin of Fàtima, are devout Catholics. Over 50% of the population claim to attend mass regularly, but it wasn't always the case. A province of the Roman Empire, Portugal was later dominated by the Visigoths and then the Moors, and didn't become a Christian country until the 12th century. The great discoveries marked the heyday of the religious orders. The powerful Order of Christ owned the caravelles, and members of the Jesuit Order went with expeditions to all four corners of the earth. The late 18th and 19th centuries became difficult times for the Church, as the Jesuits were expelled and the religious orders dissolved.

ST ANTHONY OF LISBON

St Anthony is considered to be one of the first world-famous Portuguese figures, and in Lisbon he's the most revered of the popular saints. However, he's known as St Anthony of Padua and is often mistaken for an Italian. He was born in Lisbon in 1195 and, although destined for a military career, chose to follow his religious vocation.

A ZEALOUS BISHOP

You may be surprised by the names of the days of the week. In many countries they're named after celestial objects (e.g. Monday, or 'moon' day) or pagan gods (e.g. Thursday, or 'Thor's' day). In Portugal, however, they're known as *segunda*, *terça*, *quarta*, *quinta* and *sexta feira* (second day, third day etc.). Martin de Braga, a 6th-century bishop, reformed the system in order to stamp out paganism. The week begins on Sunday (*domingo*) and ends on Saturday (*sábado*).

He was a brilliant theologian and became a doctor of the church, later travelling to Morocco as an evangelist. After a terrible storm, he landed in Italy and joined the Franciscan order, where he was a peerless orator with the power to convert heretics. He had great charisma and performed miracles. He died in Padua in 1231 and was canonised a year later as St Anthony of Padua.

THE JUNE FESTIVALS

On 12 June, St Anthony's Day, the whole of Lisbon celebrates. Everyone wears the traditional costumes of their district and they walk in

procession behind the statue of St Anthony down Avenida da Liberdade, and through the narrow streets of the Alfama, carrying a candle and chanting prayers as they walk. People buy pots of lucky basil and stop at makeshift restaurants to feast on grilled sardines and peppers. St John's Day and St Peter's Day in late June provide an opportunity for further processions and celebrations.

FOOTBALL, A WHOLE NEW RELIGION

Football is probably the second most important 'religion' in the country, possibly the most important to some, and it occupies a crucial place in the media, sometimes even eclipsing politics and the economy. On evenings when important matches are being

played, the residents of the Alfama bring their televisions and chairs into the street so that they can share the excitement of the match with their neighbours, as they do on the feasts of the popular saints. Lisbon has two rival clubs, Benfica and Sporting, both of which have ardent supporters, but when it comes to beating FC Porto, the people of Lisbon are united.

THE *TOURADA*

The *tourada* also has a massive following in Portugal. Like a Spanish bullfight, a horseman first executes complicated passes to plant banderillas in the bull's neck. But the moment of truth is the *pega*. The *forcados* (men on foot) enter the ring and try and get the bull to charge, then stop him by seizing him between the horns, by the neck

and by the tail. The bull isn't killed in the Portuguese *tourada* – at least not in the bullring. It's generally slaughtered the next day, as it would be too dangerous to fight a second time. To attend a bullfight in Lisbon, contact Praça de Touros, Campo Pequeno ☎ 21 793 21 43, (seats cost 1,000–12,000esc).

Engraving by Goya

THE RIGHT SAINT TO CALL ON

According to an popular old saying, there's a saint for every event in life, so it's a good idea to know the right one to call on and the right offering to make to get their blessings.

St Anthony – lost property and marriages (offerings of various objects).

St Christopher – protection against thieves (offerings of bread).

St Bento – the birth of a child (offerings of salt).

St Mamede – breast-feeding (offerings of milk).

St Bartholomew – the growth and health of children (offerings of food).

St Martin – the protection of alcoholics (offerings of wine). If you can't find the saint you need, you can always have recourse to Our Lady (*Nossa Senhora*) for *da saude* (to get you back to health), *da cabeça* (of the head), *das febres* (of fevers), *da luz* (of light, for the partially sighted), and *dos remedios* (to cure ailments of every kind).

PORT AND OTHER WINES

The vineyards of the Douro region have had the right to produce port since 1756, and made the first *appellation contrôlée* wine in the world. In the 18th century, an English merchant came up with the idea of fortifying a local wine with brandy. This became fashionable and exports of port to England flourished.

PORT – A WEIGHTY TRADITION

The wine-making process has remained the same, even though modern vats have often replaced the old stone ones. During the fermentation of the grapes, brandy is added to create 20° alcohol. The following spring, the entire wine harvest is transported to Vila Nova de Gaia, the home of port-making, where conditions are ideal for the ageing of the wine.

QUICK GUIDE TO PORT

Not all ports are the same. According to the grapes, the year, the wine-making process and the length of time the wine is aged, the port will be very different. The colour of the grapes determines the colour of the wine. White grapes produce white port, or *porto branco*. Red grapes produce ruby port, or *porto tinto,* and tawny port, or *porto aloirado*. Depending on the origin of the grapes and the process used, the following types of port will be produced.
Blends – blends of grapes from different years and vines, aged for three years.
Quintas – ports from a single

property, aged for at least three years.
Colheitas – a selection of vintages aged in wooden casks for seven years.
Late Bottled Vintage (L.B.V) – a vintage kept for four to six years in casks before being bottled and sold.
Vintage – a vintage from an outstanding year that's kept in a cask for two years before being aged in bottles for 10 to 30 years (or more).

HOW TO DRINK PORT

Dry *branco* port is usually served chilled as an aperitif, whereas ordinary 3-year-old ruby or tawny port is drunk after a meal with cheese or dessert. Port over 10 years old is drunk as a digestif in a ceremonial atmosphere, and an L.B.V. or vintage port is for special occasions only. For an

L.B.V. and a vintage port, the bottle must be kept on its side with the label uppermost. Before it is drunk, it should be decanted and left for a few hours so that the sediment remains at the bottom.

ALL ABOUT MADEIRA

Along with port, Madeira is the most popular Portuguese wine abroad, but relatively few people know the proper way to

drink it. There are four different types. *Sercial*, the most dry, is drunk as an aperitif. *Verdelho*, which is a little less dry and amber-coloured, is also drunk as an aperitif. *Boal*, which is sweeter, goes very well with cheese. And, lastly, *Malvasia*, which is very sweet, is served as a dessert wine or digestif. All these wines are between 17·2 and 22°, and are aged for 3 to 22 years. A wine labelled *Reserva* must be at least 5 years old; a *Reserva Velha* is at least 10 years old; and a *Colheita* is at least 22 years old.

OTHER WINES

Minho is the largest *appellation contrôlée* region and the home of *vinho verde*, a young, slightly rough white wine that's drunk chilled. *Alvarinho* is one of the best-known wines. To buy it, choose a *Quinta* or regional co-operative (600–1,000esc). **Douro** is famous for port, but also offers a range of

red wines much favoured by the critics. Don't miss the *Quinta do Côtto*, the wine of the Champallimaud family of Portuguese industrialists (from 1,800esc).

Dão and the vineyards of the Serra de Estrela have been home to traditional wine-making since the 13th century. Try the old reds, such as *Dão Pipas* and *Sogrape Reserva* (1,500–4,000esc).

Bairrada has only been an *appellation contrôlée* region since 1979, but already produces renowned wines, including some reds that age very well. A *Luis Pato Vinhas Velhas* or a *Frei João Reserve* (1,800–8,000esc) is the equal of a good bordeaux.

Alentejo wines are fruity, with a high alcohol content.

AN ESSENTIAL PORT OF CALL

Coisas do Arco Do Vinho, Rua Bartolomeu Dias, Loja 7, Centro Cultural de Belém ☎ 21 361 20 31 Every day 11am–8pm, closed Mon.

Francisco Barão da Cunha and José Oliveira Azevedo both have a long-standing passion for port. They select the wines and ports on offer in their shop very carefully. You'll find the best Portuguese wines here, along with a range of accessories (glasses, corkscrews, etc.) and a choice of traditional products. On one Saturday in the month, they hold tastings in the presence of an oenologist (wine expert) or well-known wine producer.

They make a marvellous accompaniment to regional country cooking. Look for the *Redondo* and *Reguengos* co-operatives (500–2,500esc). **Ribatejo**, on the banks of the Tagus, produces good wines that are easy to drink. Try the *Casa Cadaval* cabernet sauvignon (1,200esc).

What to see

Practicalities

GETTING ABOUT

The best way to explore the city centre is on foot,

or by public transport or taxi, (which are very cheap). A car is more trouble than it's worth, given the narrow streets, the difficulty of finding your way about in some parts of the city (the Alfama and the Bairro Alto) and the virtual impossibility of finding anywhere to park (there are few underground car parks, but they're very expensive and are often full in any case).

Buses, trams (*eléctricos*) and funiculars (*eleva dores*) can be very welcome ways to get from one district to another, as the streets are sometimes very steep. If, on the other hand, you're visiting Sintra or the Costa do Estoril, forget the express trains and hire a car. Lastly, a boat ride can be a good opportunity to see the city from a different perspective (there are organised trips and regular services).

BY METRO, TRAM, *ELEVADOR* AND BUS

Since Expo '98, two new lines have been added to the metro system, and the opening of Baixa-Chiado, Cais do Sodré, Rato and Oriente stations ensures excellent cover of the city.

Expect to pay 100esc for a ticket, 800esc for a carnet of 10, 260esc for a day ticket, and 920esc for a weekly travelcard. These tickets are only valid on the metro. With over 100 buses and 6 trams, the bus and tram network is dense, pratical and picturesque.

NÃO OBLITERE
TARIFA de BORDO

0243274

VÁLIDO APENAS NA VIAGEM EM QUE FOR COMPRADO

The termini for most of the buses and trams serving the city centre are in Praça da Figueira, Praça do Comércio or Cais do Sodré in the Baixa.

The 28 tram, which crosses the city from east to west, and the no.15, which runs along the River Tagus from Praça do Comércio to Belém, are worth bearing in mind. Don't forget the *elevadores*, three funiculars (Bica, Gloria and Lavrà), and lift (Santa Justa), which are an unusual, if indispensable, way of climbing the hills of Lisbon. In general, public transport runs from 7am to midnight, with some buses and trams running until 2am.

Carris, which operates the Lisbon public transport system, offers cut-price tourist tickets valid on all forms of public transport.

These include one-day tickets (450esc), three-day tickets (1,050esc) and a *passe touristico* valid for four days (1,550esc) or seven days (2,190esc).

For occasional journeys, you can simply buy a return ticket from a Carris kiosque for 160esc (the normal price of a one-way ticket bought from the driver). Ask, too, for a plan (*planta dos transportes*), which is very useful when it comes to finding your way about. The Carris kiosks (☎ 21 363 20 44) in Praça da Figueira, Praça de Estrêla and Elevador Santa Justa, are open every day 8am-8pm).

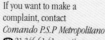

BY TAXI

Though traditionally black and green, the taxis are nearly all beige nowadays. There are plenty of them about and they're cheap. You can hail them in the street if the green light isn't on, meaning they're already occupied. There are plenty of taxi ranks, too, as well as call centres. (☎ 21 811 11 00 or 21 815 50 61). In principle, every taxi has a meter, which should read 300esc at the start of the ride. There's a 200esc surcharge if you call a taxi and a 200esc surcharge for bulky luggage.

If you want to make a complaint, contact *Comando P.S.P Metropolitano* ☎ 21 346 61 41, quoting the number of the taxi in question. For lost property enquiries, contact *Esquadra P.S.P dos Olivais* ☎ 21 853 54 03.

BY BOAT

Several regular ferry services run between Lisbon and the other bank of the Tagus. They share the landing stages of Praça do Comercio (Cais da Alfândega), Cais do Sodré and Belém and go as far as Cacilhas, Montijo and Porto Brandão. The view from the river is well worth the moderate price of the crossing (100esc). For more information, contact **Transtejo** on Cais d'Alfândega or call ☎ 21 322 40 00.

HIRING A CAR

Be very careful if you hire a car. The idea of cars as a means of mass transport has only recently been introduced to the Portuguese (the number of cars on the road has increased tenfold since 1986), and the use of rear mirrors and indicators isn't a matter of course. Portugal still holds the unenviable record for the highest number

of accidents per person in Europe. All the car hire companies are represented at the airport, and are generally open every day from 6am to midnight.

Avis ☎ 21 849 99 47
Eurodollar ☎ 21 847 06 61
Hertz ☎ 21 849 27 22

SENDING POSTCARDS AND MAKING A TELEPHONE CALL

Stamps (*selos*) are on sale at post offices and shops displaying the *Correios de Portugal* symbol (a white winged horse on a red background) and the word '*selos*'. The postal service is pretty

Portugal are among the most expensive in Europe. The best plan is to phone from the central post office, which has user-friendly opening hours and phone booths. Some public telephone boxes now take Visa and Eurocard, but they're few and far between. Otherwise you'll need to get a phone card, which you can purchase at a tobacconist's, or make sure you have plenty of small change on you.

good, and postcards generally take two or three days to reach the UK. The normal rate for postcards or letters to countries in the European Union is 95esc, and around twice that for express delivery (*correio azul*). Post offices are open Monday to Friday, 9am to 6pm. Only those in the city centre and at the airport stay open later. Praça das Restauradores Mon.-Sat. 8am-10pm; and the airport every day, 24 hrs a day.

If you make a phone call from your hotel room, find out the rates in advance, otherwise you may be in for quite a shock when you come to pay the bill. Phone calls in

To phone the UK, dial 00 44, followed by the dialling code minus the 0 (e.g. for London, dial 00 44 20) then the number you're calling. Other useful phone codes are:
Ireland: 00 353
US/Canada: 001
Australia: 0061
New Zealand: 0064

To phone a Lisbon number while you're in the city, dial the 9 figures of the number you're calling (phone numbers recently changed, so check they're still valid). To call Lisbon from another city in Portugal,

USEFUL PHONE NUMBERS

Police, [P.S.P]
☎ 21 346 61 41
Lost property (metro)
☎ 21 342 77 07
Lost property (Carris)
☎ 21 342 79 44
Emergencies Doctors rarely make home visits, so it's best to go straight to a hospital, remembering to take your E111 with you (see page 7). Treatment is only free in public hospitals. SOS ☎ 112.
Fire brigade ☎ 115 or 21 342 22 22.
Ambulances ☎ 21 942 11 11.
Clínica Médica Internacional de Lisboa ☎ 21 353 08 17 (private English-speaking doctors who will make home visits. Expect to pay 15-20,000esc).
The hospitals with emergency departments are **Estefânia** (children), Rua Jacinta Marto, **Santa Maria**, Av. Prof. Egas Moniz, and **Hospital Particular** (private), Av. Luis Bivar, 30.
British Hospital Rua Saraiva de Carvalho, 49 ☎ 21 395 50 67, (English-speaking staff) for an ambulance ☎ 21 301 77 77

dial 01. To call Lisbon from the UK, dial 00 351, followed by the number you're calling. To make a reverse charges call, dial 180 123.

To send an international telegram, dial 182.

TOURIST INFORMATION OFFICES

The main tourist information office in the city is at Palácio Foz, Praça das Restauradores ☎ 21 346 63 07, every day 9am-8pm.

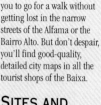

At the airport ☎ 21 849 43 23 every day 6am-2am.

Very good leaflets on the various districts of the city are available in English from the tourist information offices. Most of the employees speak English and will be happy to

you to go for a walk without getting lost in the narrow streets of the Alfama or the Bairro Alto. But don't despair, you'll find good-quality, detailed city maps in all the tourist shops of the Baixa.

SITES AND MONUMENTS

The museums and monuments are generally open on six out of seven days from 10am to 12.30pm and from 2 to 5pm, and are closed one day a week (often on Mondays). However, these opening times can vary according to the season (they close an hour later in summer) and the museum. Ask at the tourist information office.

The main museums (Arte Artiga, Gulbenkian, Jerónimos and Azulejo) are closed on Mondays and holidays.

CHANGING MONEY

You can change money over the counter at almost all the large banks (open Monday to Friday, 8.30am to 3pm). When you're going for the weekend, it's probably best to withdraw escudos using an international credit card, such as Visa, Eurocard, Mastercard or American Express. All the cash machines in the city take foreign cards and even let you choose your language. Look for the blue and white *Multibanco* sign and the initials MB. It's usually possible to withdraw up to 40,000esc a day.

Companhia Carris de Ferro de Lisboa
Bilhete 1 Dia   430$00
015 30 97/09/28 11:17   07
Manter até final da viagem
B 0250820   IVA 5%

provide you with other information (on hotels, shows, festivals, museums, etc.). Don't hesitate to ask about anything you're interested in, as far more documentation is available than is initially offered. On the other hand, the city map you're given is difficult to use and far too general. It will enable you to locate the districts you want to visit, but won't allow

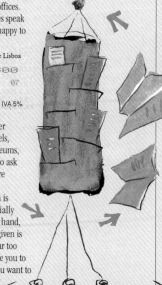

All square in the Baixa

Tthe Baixa (pronounced *Bayesha*) was entirely rebuilt after the earthquake of 1755 according to plans by the Marquês de Pombal. Known as the 'Lower City', it resembles a chessboard and is crossed by a navigable arm of the Tagus. In the 7th century BC it was the centre of vital trading activities, and nothing has changed much since – it's still the commercial heart of the city, filled with pedestrianized streets and delightful traditional shops.

2 Casa dos Bicos★
Rua dos Bacalhoeiros
☎ **21 888 48 27**

The intriguing Casa dos Bicos takes its name from the diamond-shaped stones *(bicos)* which decorate its façade. Built around 1523 by the son of the viceroy of India, it's one of the last remaining symbols of the

1 Praça do Comércio★★★

The old Palace Square, whose shady arcades are home to *alfarrabistas* (second-hand booksellers), didn't escape the 18th-century reconstruction. Surrounded by beautiful saffron yellow buildings (ministries), it opens onto both the Baixa, through a triumphal arch, and the Tagus, via a landing stage. When the offices empty at the end of the day, a dense crowd rushes for the ferries linking Lisbon to the suburbs on the other side of the river.

district's former prosperity, and was home to many noble families in the 16th century. Now restored, with another floor added, it's the head office of the National Commission for Discoveries, and is only open for exhibitions.

❸ Igreja Nossa Senhora da Conceição Velha★★
Rua da Alfândega, 112-114.

Only the 16th-century façade and portal of the church survived the earthquake. Take time to admire the classic Manueline sculptures, and look out for the one portraying the Virgin sheltering King Manuel I under her mantle.

❹ Roman excavations★★★
Fundação Banco Comercial Português
Rua dos Correeiros, 9 R/C
☎ 21 321 17 00
Guided tours
Thu. 3pm, 4pm and 5pm,
Sat. every hour 10am-5pm
Entry free.

When you push open the massive portal at the rear entrance to the Banco Comercial Português, you'll experience the Lisbon of Roman times. As soon as you

enter you'll see a paved way, with the traces of Roman chariot wheels still visible. An underground tour takes you around the remains of Roman and medieval houses as well as a commercial complex, strewn with grain silos, oil amphoras and fish salting basins. Salt fish was exported throughout the Roman empire, accompanied by *garum*, a marinade made from exotic spices. A magnificent mosaic from the 3rd-century AD also reveals the presence of thermal baths.

❺ Rua Augusta★★

This pedestrian street, with its identical façades, is the main thoroughfare of the Baixa, and was at the heart of Pombal's plans. It's always packed (except on Sundays), and from the first ray of morning sunlight its terraces are full. Streets in one direction bear the names of the trades (Rua dos Sapateiros – shoemakers, Rua dos Correeiros – saddlers, etc.), while the streets that cross them are named after their patron saints. When the Baixa was built, its craftsmen were grouped in corporations, and this is still true today – just look at Rua do Ouro (goldsmiths) or Rua da Prata (silversmiths).

❻ Elevador de Santa Justa★★★
Every day 8am-8pm
Charge for lift (160esc).

The plans for this lift are said to have been drawn up by a disciple of Eiffel (of Tower

fame) at the beginning of the 20th century. The style is

❼ A Ginjinha★★
Largo S. Domingos, 8.

This tiny bar only serves cherry brandy (*ginjinha*), and is almost always full. The Portuguese love to drink *ginjinha* before meals, and its almost a ritual to have it as an aperitif with friends at any time of day. Don't drink too much, though, as it's fairly alcoholic!

quite unmistakable, with iron latticework on the outside and a wooden interior with seats and even a lift attendant, who whisks you up to a platform above the Baixa. To prove its strength, the king once rode on horseback across the gangway linking the lift to the Chiado in front of an amazed crowd. Sadly, the bridge is now deemed dangerous and is closed to the public. However, you can still reach the bar terrace by the spiral staircases above the lift, from where you can get a marvellous view of the sunset over the Baixa and the castle.

❽ Manuel Tavares★★
Rua da Betesga, 1 A/B
☎ **21 342 42 09**
Mon.-Fri. 9.30am-7.30pm,
Sat. 9am-1pm.

The shelves of this small grocer's shop are overflowing with goods, and sweets sit side-by-side with regional specialities. It's a great place to buy culinary souvenirs, with *queijo da Serra* (ewe's cheese) at 3,700esc a kilo/ 2·2lb; *Beira Baixa* (uncooked ham) at 2,100esc a kilo/2·2lb; *choriço* (Alentéjo charcuterie) at 1,600esc a kilo/2·2lb; pig's trotters;

and *Alheiras de Mirandela* (sausages).

❾ Confeitaria Nacional★★
Praça da Figueira, 18-B
☎ **21 342 44 70**
Mon.-Fri. 8am-8.30pm,
Sa.t 8am-2pm.

This is one of the oldest patisseries in Lisbon, and *bolos* and *pasteis* have been made here since 1829. As they are brought out of the oven, you're likely to find the delicate aroma of vanilla which they give off very hard to resist.

❿ Hospital das Bonecas★
Praça da Figueira, 7
☎ **21 342 85 74**
Mon.-Fri. 10am-7pm,
Sat. 10am-1pm.

This long, narrow shop sells rag dolls which are made on the premises, as well as all kinds of doll's accessories, including clothes, hats and shoes. The smart dresses made of velvet and lace are rather expensive, but are quite beautiful. It's also a doll's hospital where you can get your broken dolls repaired.

⓫ Estação du Rossio★
Praça Dom João da Câmara

⓬ Casa Macàrio ★★
Rua Augusta, 272-276
☎ **21 342 90 29**
Mon.-Fri. 9am-7pm,
Sat. 9am-1pm.

If you like the smell of freshly roasted coffee, pop along to Macàrio, which has imported coffee since the turn of the 20th century. It offers an incredible variety of coffees from the former Portuguese colonies, Brazil, the São Tomé Islands (Africa) and Timor (Indonesia), at an average price of 1,800esc a kg/2.2lb. You'll also find the oldest port in Lisbon here, and possibly the port of your dreams, a *Colheita*, an *L.B.V* or a *Vintage* (see page 30). After that it's all a question of price (from 15,000esc for a 35-year-old *Colheita* to 25,000esc for a *Vintage* of the same age).

Between Praça du Rossio and Praça dos Restauradores stands Rossio station. The façade is definitely in the Manueline style, yet the building only dates from 1887, a time when neo-Manueline pastiches (almost perfect imitations of the original) were in favour.

⓭ Avenida da Liberdade ★★

This grand part of Lisbon may remind you of Paris and the Champs-Élysées, with its rows of plane trees, fountains and luxury shops, including Armani, Calvin Klein, Ermenegildo Zegna, Hugo Boss, Helmut Lang and Dolce & Gabbana. Unique pieces by John Galliano and Alexandre

McQueen are on display at O Espaço (no. 224A). Don't miss the Art Deco façade of the **Eden Theatre** by the Portuguese architect Cassiano Branco (1937), which now houses the **Virgin Megastore** and Hotel Orion. This fine avenue ends in **Praça Marquês de Pombal**, where Pombal's statue takes pride of place.

⓮ Coliseu dos Recreios ★
Rua das Portas de Santo Antão, 92-104
☎ **21 346 19 97.**

⓯ Sociedade de Geografia de Lisboa ★★
Rua das Portas de Santo Antão, 100
☎ **21 342 54 01**
Mon., Wed., Fri. 11am-1pm, 3-5pm
Entry free
Enrol in advance.

In Rua das Portas de Santo Antão, which is full of tourist restaurants, you can't miss the large white building of the

Coliseu, a former theatre that's now a rock and pop venue. Next door to it, the Lisbon Geographical Society is home to a number of treasures, including a painting depicting Vasco da Gama's arrival in India, a ceremonial room designed by Eiffel, and art collections from the former Portuguese colonies.

⓰ Praça Dom Pedro IV or Rossio ★★

Known by the inhabitants of Lisbon as Praça Rossio, until the 18th century this square was the setting for markets, bullfights and executions. In the middle of the square stands the statue of Dom Pedro, the ex-king of Portugal and Brazil, although some say it really depicts Maximilian, Emperor of Mexico. Pause for a while in front of the **Tabaccaria Monaco** (at no. 21). The azulejo tiles of the façade represent animals straight out of the fables of La Fontaine, and the Art Deco style of the interior has been perfectly preserved.

Chic shopping in the Chiado

For the second time the Chiado is rising from the ashes. First rebuilt after the 1755 earthquake, it became a district boasting chic shops and meeting-places favoured by bohemian artists. The quarter was again destroyed, this time by fire in 1988, and has been carefully restored in accordance with the 18th-century plans. Today, the district is gradually recovering its identity.

❶ Praça Luís de Camões★

This square, situated on the borders of the Bairro Alto, is the ideal place for a short break in the shade of its pine trees. Stop and watch the toing and froing of the trams, but don't miss the statue of Camões, the famous author of *Os Luciados* in the centre of the square. In June, the square is a lively setting both

night and day for historical reconstructions, concerts and public dances.

❷ Rua Garett★★

This pedestrian street, for a long time a shopping mecca, is now seeking a new identity. The district's makeover was only completed in 2000, when the Grandes Armazens do Chiado, a luxury shopping centre, finally opened its doors. The traditional shops, such as

Casa Pereira, which sells tea and coffee, and Parisem Lisboa, which is known for its household linen, are so far resisting the invasion of the international franchises.

❸ Museu do Chiado★
Rua Serpa Pinto, 4
☎ 21 343 21 48
Wed.-Sun. 10am-6pm,
Tue. 2-6pm, closed Mon.
Entry charge.

The restoration carried out by the architect Jean-Michel Willmotte has considerably enhanced this former monastery by revealing the brick ovens in which the monks once baked their bread. The collections inside are devoted to 19th-century Portuguese painting, and the sculpture rooms include

❹ A BRASILEIRA ★★
Rua Garett, 120
☎ **21 346 95 41**
Every day 8am-2am.

This famous café is situated at the heart of the district in which the poet Fernando Pessoa was born, and a statue of him stands on the terrace. Until the 1950s, writers and artists used to meet here, and in the late 1960s it was frequented by opponents of the Salazar regime. Today it's still the favourite meeting-place of painters, designers and other residents of the district, as it combines the charm of an Art Nouveau interior with a lively atmosphere.

works by Rodin. The museum also stages regular exhibitions of contemporary art.

❺ Vista Alegre ★★
Largo do Chiado, 28
☎ **21 346 14 01**
Mon.-Fri. 9.30am-7pm,
Sat. 9am-1pm.

❻ Casa Alegre
Rua Ivens, 58
☎ **21 347 58 33**
Mon.-Fri. 9.30am-7pm,
Sat. 9am-1pm.

Founded near Aveiro in 1824, the most famous Portuguese porcelain factory now has

two shops in the district. One sells the more traditional lines, alongside some attractive modern designs in shades of yellow and blue, with prices that are much more affordable than those of Limoges porcelain. The other outlet is devoted to a new range of china for everyday use, which features imaginative, modern designs, very bright colours and even lower prices. A dinner plate costs around 1,070esc, and a dessert plate around 710esc.

❼ O Chá do Carmo

Largo do Carmo, 21
☎ **21 342 13 05**
Mon.-Fri. 8am-8pm,
Sat. 10am-8pm.

This tea room has opened recently opposite the ruined Igreja do Carmo, whose nave collapsed during mass in the 1755 earthquake. Never

reconstructed or demolished, the church stands as a moving testament to the disaster and is closed to the public. Fortunately the Chá do Carmo is open for business, and is well worth a visit. Try one of the delicious homemade tarts with a cup of tea or hot chocolate. It's a good idea to arrive early for lunch as it's very popular with the locals.

❽ A 19TH-CENTURY AZULEJO FAÇADE ★★

Largo Rafael Bordalo Pinheiro.

In the 19th century, azulejo tiles were used to decorate the façades of shops, markets, stations and private houses and the façade of the Largo Bordalo Pinheiro is a good example. Executed by Luis Ferreira das Tabuletas, the most famous artist of the day, the style is naive, with the trompe-l'œil figures on a yellow background representing the four elements and seasons.

Day and night in the Bairro Alto

The Bairro Alto is one of the most picturesque and relaxed districts in the city, with its steep streets, family-run *tascas* (bistros) and craft workshops. It has also recently become the chosen location of young designers and interior decoration shops. By night, it vibrates to the rhythm of its bars, restaurants, *fado* clubs and discos.

❶ Casa das Velas do Loreto★★★
Rua do Loreto, 53-55
☎ 21 342 53 87
Mon.-Fri. 9am-7pm,
Sat. 9am-1pm.

Since its foundation on 14 July 1789, the Loreto candle factory has belonged to the Sà Pereira family, and it's still run using jealously guarded secrets. The candle moulds are all carefully made to the highest quality, and the shop is a great place to buy presents. It's hard to resist the novel embroidered candles or the floating candles created in the shape of flowers and leaves. The honey candles are simple but fragrant, and one is enough to perfume an entire room.

❷ Fátima Lopes★★
Rua da Atalaia, 36
☎ 21 324 05 78
Shop: Mon.-Sat. 11am-7pm,
Bar: Mon.-Sat. 10pm-4am.

Some people see the decline of the district as inevitable, in spite of the plans for urban renewal which are currently being implemented. However, the designer Fátima Lopes is optimistic and at the start of 1999 she staged the grand opening of her new shop, workshop, modelling agency and bar (over 1,500m²/16,000sqft

in all), which are decorated in her favourite colours of violet and mauve. She has also added a line of relatively affordable accessories to clothes that are as avant-garde as ever.

❸ Da Natura★★
Rua da Rosa, 162 A
☎ 21 346 60 81
Mon.-Fri. 11am-7pm, Sat. 11am-1.30pm, 3-6pm.

Da Natura has a marvellous selection of furniture and objects from the former Portuguese colonies (India, Mozambique, etc.), as well as masks from Mali, carpets from Afghanistan, and fabrics and totems from Fiji. If you love ethnic art and crafts, then make sure you don't miss this shop.

❹ Restaurant Pap'açorda★★★

Rua da Atalaia, 57
Mon.-Sat. 12.30-2.30pm, 8-11.30pm, closed Sun.

One of the most famous and trendiest restaurants in Lisbon, Pap'açorda is well-known as the meeting-place of celebrities. Choose between the Baroque room, with its pink walls, green velvet curtains and huge crystal chandelier, and the high-tech room, with its blue decor and halogen lighting. Make sure you try the delicious house speciality, *açorda*, a type of bread soup made with onions, coriander, eggs and either shellfish or fish.

❺ Igreja de São Roque★★★
Largo Trindade Coelho
☎ 21 346 03 61
Every day 8.30am-5pm, holidays 8.30am-1pm.

The church was built by the Jesuits in 1525 and formed part of the architectural complex which included the seminary and college. Only part of this now remains and has been turned into a museum. The Capela de São João Baptista inside the church is considered to be one of the great masterpieces of 18th-century European art. This chapel, commissioned in 1742 by Dom João V, was built in Rome by over 130 artists using only the most costly and precious materials available, before being dismantled and transported to Lisbon at enormous expense on board three ships.

❼ São Pedro de Alcântara Belvedere★★
Rua de S. Pedro d'Alcântara.

❽ Elevador da Gloria★★
Calçada da Gloria.

The best way to reach this viewpoint is to use the da Gloria funicular linking Avenida da Liberdade with the Bairro Alto (see page 12). Ideally, visit in the late afternoon when the old stones of the castle and the cathedral towers are bathed in the golden evening light.

❻ La Paparrucha★★
Rua D. Pedro V, 18/20
☎ 21 342 53 33
Every day noon-2am.

With its grilled meat specialities from Patagonia, and a vast bay window offering an outstanding view, this new Argentinian restaurant is one of the most popular restaurants in Lisbon. If you want to try the delicious house speciality of Patagonian-style *cordeiro* (lamb), remember it takes seven hours to cook, so it's essential to book the day before. Otherwise, you'll still have a wide choice of grilled dishes (expect to pay 5,000–6,000esc per person).

The Alfama, medieval Lisbon

The Alfama is the old centre of the city, and historians believe it was the site of *Olisipo* (Roman Lisbon) and the heart of the later Arab city. It's the only part of the city to have survived the earthquake, and is still a popular area with anglers and craftsmen.

❶ Chafariz d'El-Rei★★
Largo do Terreiro do Trigo.

❷ Chafariz de Dentro★
Largo do Chafariz de Dentro.

The name *Alfama* comes from the Arabic word *al-hama*, meaning 'hot fountain', but sadly these are the last two *chafariz* (fountains) left in the district today. There were once natural hot springs here, and the life of the district centred around them. Until recently, the women of the area drew their drinking water from the fountains, but today they're no longer in use, despite the fact that some of the local houses still have no bathrooms and the families living in them have to use the public washhouses instead. You can see the wheat warehouses, tanneries, shipyards and foundries by

the river, while the fishermen's houses are perched on the hillside.

❸ Igreja de Santo Estevão★★
Largo de Santo Estevão
Mon.-Sat. after 4.30pm (usually).

Founded in the 12th century, the church has been remodelled several times and now has an octagonal plan unique in Lisbon. The interior is worth seeing for the choir and the very fine colourful wooden statue of St Theresa of Avila in the sacristy.

QUICK GUIDE TO A WALK IN THE ALFAMA

The names of the streets are very inviting, and the following will help you find your way round.

Beco (B. on the plan), means 'beak', and is a very narrow, winding street (e.g. Beco das Cruzes).

Calçada or **calçadinha** (C. on the plan) means roadway, and may involve a climb, which can turn out to be quite steep (e.g. Calçada de S. Miguel).

Travessa (T. on the plan) means a crossing street and is often for pedestrians only (e.g. Travessa de S. Miguel).

Escadinhas (E. on the plan), means small staircase and may involve a steep climb (e.g. Escadinhas de S. Estêvão).

Pátio (P. on the plan) means courtyard, and is generally at the end of a cul-de-sac (e.g. Patio de Lajes).

4 Páteo 13★★
Calçadinha S. Estevao, 13
☎ 21 888 23 25
Mon.-Fri. noon-3pm,
7pm-midnight.

This charming *tasca* (bistro) is typical of the Alfama. The best time to visit is from June onwards, when the tables are set up in the little square and the barbecue is in use outside. It's an ideal place to

enjoy a leisurely lunch of sardines or grilled fish with a house salad.

5 Casa do Fado and da Guitarra Portuguesa★★★
Edifício do Recinto da Praia,
Largo do Chafariz do Dentro
☎ 21 882 34 70
Tue.-Sun. 10am-5pm
Entry charge.

This museum, housed in a 19th-century former pumping station, is the first in the country to be devoted to the art of *fado* and the Portuguese guitar. It contains a number of interesting items, including gala outfits, musical instruments and archive films.

6 Rua da Judiaria★

This is the last vestige of the old Jewish quarter, which was founded in the 14th century. Although abolished by Manuel I in 1496, the door used to be closed every evening to isolate the *Judiaria* (ghetto) from the Christians.

7 Igreja and Largo de S. Miguel★★★

The charming Igreja S. Miguel, with its two white bell-towers standing out against the sky, was originally built in the 12th century, then rebuilt in 1674, and fortunately

suffered very little damage in the earthquake (see page 24). The Largo S. Miguel is an enchanting street, especially at dusk.

8 Restaurant Malmequer Bemmequer★★
Rua de S. Miguel, 25
☎ 21 887 65 35
Wed.-Sun., noon-3pm,
7-10pm.

This pretty restaurant is located only a few minutes from Igreja de São Miguel, and is a pleasant place to stop for a break and sample some typical Portuguese dishes.

Belém, the gateway to the ocean

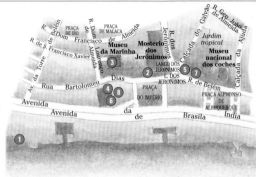

Belém, which is
Portuguese
for 'Bethlehem',
is one of Lisbon's
most historic
areas. The district
has witnessed countless naval departures and
triumphant returns, and is a tribute to the exploits
of the sailors who set sail to discover the New World.

❶ Torre de Belém★★
Av. de Brasilia
☎ 21 362 00 34
Every day except Mon.
Oct.-Apr. 10am-5pm,
May-Sep. 10am-6pm
Entry charge.

When the city became an
obligatory port of call on
the international trading
routes, a defence tower was
needed for the port. The
building work, directed by
Diogo de Boitaca, the
architect of the Mosteiro dos
Jéronimos, was completed in
1520. The whole monument
is a reminder of the golden
age of discovery, decorated
with ropes knotted round the
building, armillary spheres,
crosses of the Order of Christ
and a few exotic animals
(including a rhinoceros).

❷ Mosteiro dos Jerónimos ★★★ and Igreja Santa Maria ★★★
Praça do Império
☎ 21 362 00 34
Every day except Mon.
Oct.-Apr. 10am-5pm,
May-Sep. 10am-6.30pm
Entry charge for cloister,
church free.

Built by order of Manuel I
(1495–1521) on the site of
the chapel of Nossa Senhora
de Restelo, where sailors
prayed before setting out on
voyages, the monument is
grandiose in terms of its
dimensions (with its
300m/330yd façade), the

time it took to build (150
years) and its cost (5% of the
annual foreign trading
income of the period, or
70kg/154lb of gold). The
monastery was entrusted to
the monks of St Jeremy with
the mission of praying for the
king and sailors. Don't miss
the tombs of Vasco da Gama
and Luís de Camões in the
entrance of the church, and
the vault and superb pillars
decorated with plant motifs
inside. The cloister galleries,
refectory and high choir
stalls are marvels of the
Manueline style.

❸ Museu da Marinha ★★
Praça do Império
☎ 21 362 00 100

Every day except Mon.
10am-5pm
Entry charge.

Greeted by a vast map of the great discoveries, the museum is packed with fascinating artefacts, including navigational instruments, naval uniforms, maps and model ships. In the shop you'll find reproductions of maps (2,000–3,000esc), 17th-century astrolabes (13,000esc), and caravelles in bottles (3,000–9-000esc) or in kit form (20,000esc).

❹ Centro Cultural de Belém★
Praça do Império
☎ **21 361 24 00**
Every day 11am-8pm.

The Centro Cultural was originally built for the six months of Portugal's

European Presidency. It resembles a huge kasbah on the outside and houses two large exhibition and concert halls, some shops and, since May 1999, the Museu do Design. Enjoy the marvellous view from the terrace over a drink in the cafeteria or dinner in the **A Comenda** restaurant.

❺ Especiarias finas★
Largo dos Jerónimos 4
☎ **21 362 33 77**
Every day 10am-6pm.

This is the perfect shop for those who love crafts, with embroidered tablecloths from Madeira and the north (a 2m/6ft 6in square tablecloth and six napkins costs 25,000esc), typical Alentéjo tableware (2,000–12,000esc according to size) and handpainted azulejo tiles (14,500esc for a panel of six). The shop will deliver throughout Europe (15% extra).

❻ Kà, objectos com alma★★★
C.C.B. Praça do Império
☎ **21 364 82 37**
Every day 11am-8pm.

Filled with original creations by young Portuguese artists, you can buy contemporary glass and wooden and ceramic decorative objects here at affordable prices. These include trays, plates, glasses, vases, chess sets, sculptures, carpets and modern azulejo tiles.

❼ Antiga Pastelaria de Belém★★★
Rua Belém 84
☎ **21 363 74 23**
Every day 8am-11pm.

Make sure this place is high on your list. The famous Belém *pasteis* are as creamy as can be. Eat them fresh from the oven with a dusting of cinnamon and icing sugar in one of the azulejo-lined rooms. There's plenty of atmosphere on a Sunday, but you sometimes have to queue.

❽ Museu do Design★★
Centro Cultural de Belém, Galeria Cruzeiro do Sul
☎ **21 361 24 00**
Every day 11am-8pm
Entry charge.

With this museum, Lisbon has acquired a design collection of international stature. Located in the Centro Cultural de Belém, it houses 600 objects presented by the collector Francisco Capelo from all over the world and covering the period from 1937 to the present day. Made of plastic, fibreglass and metal, they reflect developments in a century devoted to design and the industrialisation of objects. Alongside the great classics, you'll find many unknown works by Portuguese artists such as Álvaro Siza Vieira and Pedro Silva Dias.

The Castelo, or the fortified town

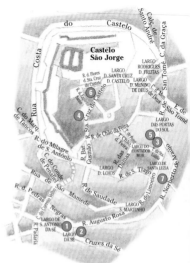

Castelo São Jorge

The stunning silhouette of the Castelo dominates the whole of the Baixa. Although all that remains of the original castle are a few of its towers, it is a pleasant place to wander around and is worth the climb for the stunning views alone. The area also boasts a fortified cathedral and the old Santa Cruz district.

❶ Igreja de São Antonio and museu★
Largo de S. Antonio da Sé
☎ 21 886 04 47
Church: every day 9am-5pm
Museum: Tue.-Fri. 10am-1pm, 2-4pm. Entry charge.

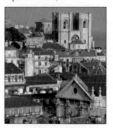

This church was built on the site of St Anthony's birthplace, and houses his statue which is borne in procession through the streets of the Alfama on his saint's day (see page 28). The adjacent museum, which documents his life, is also worth a visit.

❷ The Sé ★★
Largo da Sé
Every day 9am-5pm
Entry free (charge for cloisters and sacristy).

Lisbon's cathedral, called the Sé, has a solid, fortress-like appearance. Soon after the reconquest of Lisbon from the Moors, King Afonso Henriques (1128–1185), the founder of the Portuguese state, ordered it to be built on the site of the former mosque. It has since undergone many alterations, but has retained its 12th-century Romanesque towers. The interior is austere and quite bare except for the baptismal fonts, in which

St Anthony is said to have been baptised, and the relics of St Vincent, the patron saint of the city.

❸ Museu de Artes Decorativas★★★
Largo das Portas do Sol, 2
☎ 21 886 21 83
Every day 10am-5pm, closed Tue.
Entry charge.

The museum is housed in the former mansion of the viscounts of Azurara. In 1947 it was bought by Ricardo Espírito Santo Silva, a Portuguese banker and patron of the arts, who restored it in the style of an aristocratic residence and filled it with his private collections. It is an excellent example of a typical 18th-century mansion, with azulejo panels and painted wooden ceilings, superb Indo-Portuguese furniture, 17th- and 18th-century Arraiolos carpets and a collection of Chinese porcelain. It is actually run as a museum school, whose purpose is to preserve the decorative arts and their traditional techniques, and if you are lucky you may see the foundation's bookbinding workshop in action.

❹ Castelo de São Jorge★★★
Costa do Castelo.

According to legend, the Romans laid the first stones of the Castelo de São Jorge, and this strategic site was later chosen by the Visigoths and Moors as a site for their fortresses. In 1147, Afonso Henriques conquered Lisbon and turned the Moorish castle into a royal palace, but after the transfer of the court from the castle to the banks of the Tagus under Manuel I (1495–1521), the castle fell into ruin, later serving as military quarters and a prison. All that remains of Afonso's castle today is a room with Gothic arches and some watchtowers, but take time to stroll around the gardens and ramparts as there's a marvellous panoramic view over the whole of Lisbon from the castle.

❺ Cerca Moura★
Largo das Portas do Sol, Loja 4
☎ 21 887 48 59
Every day 10pm-2am, closed Sun.

This small and intimate bar located beside the Portas do Sol *miradouro* is a good place to stop for a drink or a bite to eat. The dish of the day is always tasty and very good value. From here you can admire the stunning view of the monastery of St Vincent and the white cupola of Santa Engracia, as well as the statue of St Vincent who holds in his hands a ship flanked by two crows.

❻ Antiga Casa do Castelo★★★
Rua Santa Cruz do Castelo, 15,
☎ 21 888 05 08
Every day 10am-7pm.

This wonderful craft shop, in the picturesque Santa Cruz do Castelo district, is run by Marsha, a friendly American woman, who will show you around her shop and share her

❼ MIRADOURO DE SANTA LUZIA★★★
Largo de Santa Luzia.

Opposite the church of Santa Luzia there's a charming garden. Under its arcades, the locals play card games, indifferent to the tourists who stop off on their way to the castle. From the viewpoint, you'll have a marvellous view of the rooftops of the Alfama, the white bell-towers of the church of S. Miguel and the Straw Sea – the name given to the Tagus due to the golden reflections of the sunlight on the water.

passion for Portuguese crafts. She travels to every corner of the country, choosing all the stock herself, including ceramic dolls from Estremoz, azulejo tiled mirrors, Alentéjo ceramics and raw cotton household linen. Everything is affordable and you'll find an incredible quantity of souvenirs for under 2,000esc.

The Fundação Calouste Gulbenkian and the avenidas, another Lisbon

The wide, serene, palm-lined *avenidas* seem far from the bustling crowds of the Baixa. Discover the formal Parque Eduardo VII, visit the Fundação Calouste Gulbenkian, the great cultural centre of Lisbon, or peruse the fine shop windows of the *avenidas*.

❶ Parque Eduardo VII★★

This 400,000m²/4,300,000sqft park in the heart of Lisbon was renamed in 1903 to honour King Edward VII, who had visited the city that year. The two main attractions are the enormous tropical glasshouses – the *estufa fria* (temperate house), whose fountains, pools and exotic

plants form a cool oasis, and the cacti-filled *estufa quente* (hothouse).

❷ Fundação Calouste Gulbenkian★★★

Av. da Berna, 45
☎ 21 795 02 36
Tue.-Sun. 10am-5pm
Entry charge except Sun.

❸ Museu d'Arte Moderna Calouste Gulbenkian★★

Rua Dr. Nicolau Bettencourt
☎ 21 793 51 31
Tue.-Sun. 10am-5pm
Entry charge.

The Fundação Calouste Gulbenkian is the cultural centre of Lisbon. Set in its own park, which contains sculptures by Rodin and Moore, it features a museum, galleries and concert halls. The Classical and Oriental art

section of the museum includes some wonderful Egyptian exhibits, as well as Chinese porcelain and Persian textiles and carpets, while the European art section houses medieval manuscripts, 14th-century ivory triptychs, works by old Masters and French Impressionists and an extraordinary Lalique

Mr 5%

Calouste Gulbenkian had an extraordinary life. As a child growing up in Turkey, he would use his pocket money to go bargain hunting in the markets, unearthing rare pieces of art and displaying an early flair for business. In 1888 he entered his father's oil business, and in 1920, on the discovery of oilfields in Iraq, he negotiated a 5% commission on their future production and made a personal fortune. Nick-named 'Mr 5%', he found himself at the head of a colossal empire and devoted himself to his passion for art, particularly Chinese porcelain, Persian art and Western painting. He travelled the world, skilfully negotiating with art dealers, even buying treasures from the Soviet Hermitage Museum after the Russian Revolution. In 1942 he auctioned himself to the European nations. Portugal offered him a palace and tax exemption in return for his collections, which were bequeathed to the State on his death in 1955.

jewellery room. Across the park lies the Museu d'Arte Moderna, founded in 1983, which displays works by Maria Vieira da Silva, Paula Rego and Almada Negreiros, as well as talented young artists, such as Rui Chafes and Pedro Proença.

❹ Praça de Touros★
Campo Pequeno
☎ 21 793 66 01
May-Sep.

The brick-red cupolas which emerge from Campo Pequeno square signify the Lisbon

bullring. Built in 1892, the building imitates Moorish art and reproduces its more symbolic aspects. From April to September you can see *touradas* (see page 29) here.

❺ Avenida de Roma★★

❻ Avenida Guerra Junqueiro★★

The *avenidas* have long been two of of Lisbon's most popular shopping areas. Avenida de Roma has now lost some of its attraction despite the presence of a few leading shops (Ana Salazar at no. 16E and Fátima Lopez at no. 44E);

however, Avenida Guerra Junqueiro is becoming a centre for high street shopping. You'll find a variety of items at interesting prices, including shoes and bags (Cérimonia at no. 11B and Jarda at no. 13B) and clothes (Esquina at no. 11C and Massimo at no. 18D). There's even a Marks & Spencer.

❼ Café Império★★
Av. Almirante Reis, 205ABC
☎ 21 847 60 52
Every day 7am-11pm.

Housed in a former cinema, this is one of the oldest grills in the city. Although the decor is rather old-fashioned, people come from all over the city to eat the *bife da casa*, a steak dish renowned for its delicious sauce.

❽ Atrium Saldanha★★
Praça Duque de Saldanha
Every day 10am-10pm.

This new shopping centre, designed by Ricardo Bofil, has over 25,000m²/270,000sqft of shops, bars and restaurants. Its opening marked the return of the district to its original role as the nerve centre of an active modern city, and it was intended primarily for the district's businesspeople.

Príncipe Real, bargains at any price

The land around the Praça do Príncipe Real has had a number of owners since the early 15th century, when the Marquês de Alegrete made plans to build a palace here. Sold to the College of Jesuits as a site for a monastery, and later requisitioned as a military camp, it was finally intended to become a monumental square in the 19th century, but a square of more modest proportions was finally built in 1853.

❶ Praça do Príncipe Real★★

The Praça do Príncipe Real has changed little since the end of the 19th century, and it still retains a metal kiosk and a giant *Cypressus Lusitanica*, the largest tree in Europe (the trunk measuring 25m/82ft in circumference). From its cool shade you can admire the magnificent façades of the square's palatial mansions, which today are given over to ministries and associations. Of particular note are the Palacete Anjos (a merchant's house) at no. 20/22, and the palace of the Comendador Faria (a banker) at no. 2/4, one of the first buildings in Lisbon to have a hydraulic lift.

❷ Pavilhão Cinês★★★
Rua Dom Pedro V, 89
☎ **21 342 47 29**
Every day 6pm-2am.

This is an amazing place to stop for a drink after a long walk, where you'll appreciate the comfortable sofas and pretty marquetry tables. There are several rooms with brick-red walls lined with display cabinets of Chinese porcelain, lead soldiers, electric model trains and military headgear from across the ages. The extensive menu offers an

excellent choice of drinks, including a wide selection of teas, delicious house cocktails and other alcoholic and non-alcoholic beverages. There's also a good snack menu if you're feeling a bit peckish.

❸ Xairel Antiguidades★
Rua Dom Pedro V, 111
☎ 21 346 02 66
Mon.-Fri. 10am-7pm, Sat. 10am-1pm.

Compared with the luxurious shop windows of the antique dealers opposite, Xairel's looks untidy, with its jumble of 16th-century azulejos (3,000esc per tile), statues of saints, oriental figures, old rocking-horses and Chinese porcelain. If you can't find what you're looking for here, try **Carvalho & Gil**, Rua da Escola Politecnica, 31-33, ☎ 21 346 94 17, open every day 9am-7pm, Sat. 9am-1pm, or **Quintela & Andrade**, 39, ☎ 21 342 49 64, open every day 10am-7pm, Sat. 11am-1pm.

❹ A Cortiça★
Rua da Escola Politecnica, 4
Mon.-Fri. 10am-1pm, 3-7pm, Sat. 10am-1pm.
Thanks to the *Cortica* (cork) oaks of Alentéjo, Portugal is one of the world's major cork producing countries,

supplying two-thirds of the cork used worldwide. Step inside this old-fashioned little shop and find out just what can be done with this versatile material, that not only keeps your wine in its bottle, but can also protect object from heat and keep items cool.

❺ Casa dos Tapetes de Arraiolos ★★★
Rua da Imprensa Nacional, 116E
☎ 21 396 33 54
Mon.-Fri. 9.30am-1pm, 3-7pm, Sat. 9.30am-1pm.
This shop specialises in the beautiful Arraiolos carpets, which originated in the Arab communities who sought refuge at Arraiolos in Alentéjo after being expelled from Lisbon's *mouraria* in the late 15th century. Inspired by the designs of ancient Persia, they are executed in cross-stitch using woollen threads on a linen or hemp weft, and are more like tapestries than carpets. They retain the strict sequencing of the motifs of their Arab origins, with a central medallion (*centro*), which is totally different from the rest of the carpet, a main section (*campo*) and a frieze (*barra*). Each carpet takes between three

and six months to produce, and they are usually made in shades of blue, yellow ochre, green or rust.

❻ PRAÇA DAS FLORES★★
Follow the slope, making your way down the steep Rua de S. Marçal, and you'll arrive at one of the most evocative squares in Lisbon – Praça das Flores. You'll suddenly find yourself in a wonderfully peaceful square where local people relax on the benches in the shade reading their newspapers or watch the little fountain play while they listen to the laughter of the children as they enjoy playing on the swings.

São Bento and Estrêla, an inspired district

A large number of monasteries and convents were established between Estrêla and São Bento from the 16th century onwards, but on 28 May 1834 this all changed when a law signed by Pedro IV abolished all religious orders. The monks and nuns were turned out, their buildings were taken over by the State, and their property was auctioned off. Today this affluent district is home to craftsmen and antique dealers.

❶ Basílica da Estrêla★★★
Praça da Estrêla
Mon.-Sat. 8am-7pm,
Sun. 9am-7pm.

This great basilica was built on the orders of Queen Maria I (1777–1816), who dedicated it to the Virgin Mary as thanks for having blessed her with a son. The gigantic building, which took over 15 years to complete, testifies to the queen's marked taste for the Baroque style, and contains her tomb as well as some beautiful coloured marbles.

❷ Jardim da Estrêla★★

If you want a respite from the heat, take a walk in the Jardim da Estrêla, just opposite the basilica. Here you can find the *coreto*, a small metal kiosk once used for public dances and lovers' trysts.

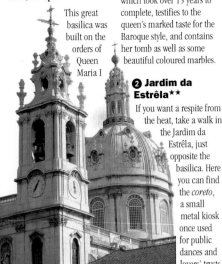

❸ Palácio da Assembléia Nacional de São Bento★

This former 16th-century abbey became the parliament in the 19th century when the Benedictine order was dissolved. Unfortunately, the former monastery has now been replaced by a charmless neo-Classical building, which today houses the Palácio da Assembléia Nacional (the Portuguese House of Commons).

❹ São Bento 34★★
Rua de S. Bento, 34
☎ 21 395 15 40.

Venture inside this bookshop, even if you don't want to buy any books, and you'll find an attractive art gallery with permanent exhibitions of

ceramics, photographs and paintings, as well as a charming tea room whose brick walls and stone vaults are reminiscent of an old convent. It's a pleasant and affordable place for a quick bite to eat, serving salads, savoury tarts, delicious home-made desserts and natural fruit juices. A complete meal won't cost more than 1,500esc.

❺ Rua de São Bento★★

Rua de São Bento is long and rises steeply from the Palácio da Assembléia Nacional to Largo do Rato. In this affluent area you'll find a wide variety of craft workshops (wooden objects in particular), second-hand shops and antique dealers of high-quality and expensive goods. If you love old objects, try **Canapé**, no. 293-308, ☎ 21 397 28 39, open Mon.-Fri. 10am-1pm, 3-7pm, Sat. 10am-1pm. If you prefer thirties styles try **Nobre**, no. 224 and 386/388, ☎ 21 396 12 27, Mon.-Fri. 10am-1pm, 3-7pm,

Sat. 10am-1pm. Bargain hunters will love **Brique à Braque de S. Bento**, no. 542, ☎ 21 390 70 01, open Mon.-Fri. 10am-1pm, 3-7pm, Sat. 10am-1pm. And finally, if you like beautiful objects, try **Ricardo Hogan**, no. 281, ☎ 21 395 41 02, Mon.-Fri. 10.30am-1pm, 3-7pm, Sat. 11am-1pm.

❻ Deposito da Marinha Grande★★
Rua de S. Bento, 418 and 420
☎ 21 396 30 96
Mon.-Fri. 9am-1pm, 3-7pm, Sat. 9am-1pm.

These two shops are the outlets of the Vidrivima de Marinha Grande factory, situated 100km/63 miles north of Lisbon, where glass has been made by traditional methods for over 100 years. In both shops you will find elaborately worked glass in many different forms — polished, matt and coloured. In the first shop, you'll find the blue cocktail service for

which it's famous (around 400–600esc a glass) as well as pretty frosted glass candlesticks (for around 800–1,000esc each). The second shop has unique pieces by Portuguese artists in original shapes and bright colours (from 12,000esc).

❼ Casa de Nossa Senhora do Amparo (Vicentinas tearoom)★★★
Rua de S. Bento, 700
☎ 21 388 70 40
Shop: Mon.-Fri. 9am-1pm, 3-7pm
Tearoom: Mon.-Sat. 4-7pm.

From the outside, it's impossible to guess what lies behind the window of this shop, which is filled with religious objects. Uninformed passers-by continue on their journeys believing it to be just a convent, and although they could be said to be correct, in the afternoon those in the know begin to gather round the door at around 4.30pm, when the *Vicentinas* tearoom opens for service. This popular tearoom is always busy, and it's well known locally that the sisters make the most heavenly pastries. Make sure you get here early, however, as they're produced in limited quantities only .

Luxurious Lapa

L apa grew in opulence in the 19th century, when the wealthy English inhabitants of Lisbon moved here seeking a quiet refuge away from the bustling city centre. Rich with grand mansions and luxurious palaces, it is now home to the wealthy Portuguese middle classes.

❶ Museu Nacional de Arte Antiga★★★
Rua das Janelas Verdes, 9
☎ 21 396 41 51
Wed.-Sun. 10am-5pm,
Tue. 2-5pm
Entry charge.

You can't miss the imposing yellow façade and huge green shutters of Portugal's national gallery. The 17th-century palace of the counts of Alvor, better known as the Palacio das Janelas Verdes

(Palace with Green Windows), is home to the finest art collection in the country and contains many Portuguese and European masterpieces (including works by Tiepolo, Dürer, Poussin and Zurbaran). It owes its reputation, however, to two remarkable paintings in particular, the altarpiece of the *Adoration of St Vincent*, painted by Nuno Gonçalves in around 1460, which depicts the important Portuguese

figures at the time of the great discoveries, and the *Temptation of St Anthony* by Hieronymus Bosch (1505), a fascinating triptych. Its caricature-like figures and multitude of symbolic details draw you into an surreal world which is quite disturbing. If you're in need of refreshment, try the **Café d'Arte** on the ground floor facing the river, or alternatively the formal gardens are ideal for a quick lunch break in summer.

❷ Casa Visconde de Sacavérn★
Rua do Sacramento à Lapa.

Thanks to the efforts of the caricaturist Rafael Bordalo Pinheiro, the fashion for azulejos in relief developed in the late 19th century, with naturalistic decorative elements including flowers,

fruit and leaves. Don't miss the the beautiful residence of the Viscount of Sacavérn, one of the finest examples of this exuberant style. The façade is a jumble of decoration including Manueline ropes, traditional azulejos and tiles formed in the shape of bunches of grapes and apples.

❸ O Acontecimento★
Rua das Trinas, 129 R/C
☎ 21 397 71 38
Mon.-Sat. 12.30-3pm, 8.30-11pm.

This new restaurant has opened in the splendid patrician residence that houses the Clube dos Jornalistas. It's a unique opportunity to see inside this charming house, which has been completely renovated from top to bottom, and to enjoy one of the city's most marvellous gardens. The chef, Juan Pulvinet, has just arrived from Barcelona and is well-known for his elegant, creative cuisine that's full of rustic, southern European flavours. An ideal place to have dinner.

❹ Companhia Inglesa★★
Rua da Bela Vista à Lapa, 88
☎ 21 396 19 77
Mon.-Fri. 10.30am-7.30pm, Sat. 1.30-7.30pm.

The wooden furniture here is a marvel of simplicity and elegance, although a little heavy to transport home. Beautifully designed, you're sure to be won over

by the natural tones, pure lines and simple but tasteful objects. Among the temptations on offer are colourful ceramic plates, table mats, fabric flowers, photograph frames and wicker baskets, and all at very affordable prices.

❻ PHONING THE OLD-FASHIONED WAY

At the start of the 20th century, Lisbon's transport and communications network was run by the English. The buses were all English double deckers and the first telephone boxes were red, made to the classic English design. One of them can still be seen today in Largo Dr. J. Figueiredo in Lapa.

❺ Aconchego★★
Travessa St. Antonio Santos, 26 A
☎ 21 60 70 27
Mon.-Fri. 10am-1pm, 3-7pm, Sat. 10am-1pm (closed Sat. 15 Jun.-15 Sep.).

This unique fabric shop is the only place where you can find the marvellous Alcobaça chintzes. In the 16th century, sailors brought back precious fabrics in fabulous colours from India, and in the 18th century they began to make these brilliant chintzes in Alcobaça, where they are still made to this day. For curtains, allow twice the width of the window by the drop of fabric required, allowing for turnings and pattern repeats (around 2,400esc a metre/39in for fabric 150cm/59in wide). For a square table (100cm/39in square), allow 1·5m/1²/3yd of fabric, or alternatively you can buy a ready-made tablecloth for around 3,000esc.

Campo de Ourique and Amoreiras

The Campo de Ourique is famous in Lisbon for its *panificação* (bread making), and still has a large number of working bakeries today, as well as a good range of small, specialist shops. Nearby, the ultramodern Centro Comercial das Amoreiras offers a more popular but less traditional shopping experience.

❶ Stop do Bairro★★
Rua Tenente Ferreira Durão 55A
☎ **21 388 88 56.**

This quaint little bistro (the quintessential *tasquinha*), has been a feature of the district for over 20 years. Its owner, Sr. João, will greet you like an old friend and even if you don't understand his jokes it really doesn't matter, as the bistro couldn't be more authentic or the owner more friendly. The cuisine is delicious and the *arroz de tamboril* (monkfish and rice)

and *pato à antiga* (duck) have made the bistro's name. Sample them by ordering a *meia dose* (a half portion, which is more than enough for one), and you'll have an excellent dinner for less than 2,000esc per person.

❷ Casa and restaurant Fernando Pessoa★★★
Rua Coelho Rocha, 16/18
☎ **21 396 81 90 (museum),**
☎ **21 397 11 79 (restaurant)**
Museum: Mon.-Sat. 10am-6pm, Thu. 1-8pm (entry free),
Restaurant: Mon.-Sat. 10am-midnight.

This was the last home of Fernando Pessoa, one of Lisbon's great writers, who rented a small room here for the last fifteen years of his life. The building has since been renovated and now houses some of Pessoa's personal belongings, as well as a well-stocked library and a poetry society. You can enjoy a meal *al fresco* in the poetical setting of the rear courtyard, where the simple set meal includes a dish of the day and a few specialities

such as *bife à Fernando Pessoa* (beef steak), as well as a dessert buffet for under 1,500esc a person.

❸ Loja das Viagens★★
Rua Correia Teles, 29
☎ 21 388 99 42
Mon.-Fri. 11am-12.30pm, 1.30-7pm.

Loja das Viagens reflects the spirit of the Portuguese explorers who once set out to discover the world. With a collection of Mexican furniture, Asian fabrics, and crafts and trinkets from all over the globe, there's a truly international feel here. They also sell a good selection of jewellery, unusual framed arrangements of exotic spices, straw hats, Polynesian-style artefacts and a number of other original objects as well.

❹ Centro Comercial das Amoreiras★★★
Av. Duarte Pacheco
☎ 21 381 02 00
Mon.-Sun. 10am-11pm.

On the summit of the Sétima Colina (Seventh Hill) stands the Amoreiras shopping centre with its futuristic architecture. Built in 1983 according to designs by the Portuguese architect Tomás Taveira, it was the largest shopping centre in the country until the giant Colombo centre opened.

A popular destination for families at the weekend in particular, this modern pink and blue extravaganza not only houses shops stocking all the well-known brands, but ten cinemas, sixty cafés and restaurants and a hotel too.

❺ Aqueduto das Águas Livres★★★
Calçadinha da Quintinha, Campolide,
☎ 21 815 36 30
Mar.-Nov., Mon.-Sat. 10am-6pm
Entry charge.

❻ Mãe d'Água das Amoreiras Reservoir ★★
Praça das Amoreiras
Mon.-Sat. 10am-6pm
Entry charge.

The *aqueduto* and Mãe d'Água reservoir, which were completed in 1834 after over 100 years of work, supply the city with fresh water. EPAL, the public company responsible for managing them, has just restored the two sites, and you can now walk the 941m/1,029yd of the *aqueduto*, viewing the city from a height of 65m/213ft. The Mãe d'Água reservoir, which has a capacity of 5,500m^3/195,000cuft, houses temporary exhibitions.

STILL MORE INTERIOR DECORATION

As you walk up and down the streets of Campo de Ourique, you'll come across numerous interior design shops, where you can stock up on souvenirs for the home.

❼ Companhia do Campo★★
Rua Saraiva de Carvalho, 203/205
☎ 21 85 27 36
Mon.-Fri. 10am-7.30pm, Sat. 10am-2pm.
A charming shop you can wander around looking for gift ideas.

❽ Casa★
Rua Tomás da Anunciação, 33 B,
☎ 21 95 34 88
Mon.-Sat. 10am-7pm.
The Portuguese equivalent of Habitat offers you a good choice of tableware and other decorative objects at much lower prices.

❾ Espaço Natureza★
Rua Correia Teles, 28-A
☎ 21 383 21 83
Mon.-Fri. 10am-7pm, Sat. 10am-1pm.
An eco-friendly shop stocking a good and varied selection of objects.

Outside the city walls

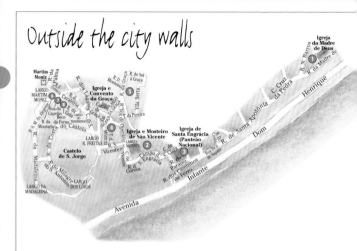

L isbon's first suburbs sprang up outside the city walls in the 13th city, but have since changed dramatically in appearance. The first major change occurred after the opening of the railway that ran alongside the Tagus in 1856, and later the city's expansion caused further alterations.

❶ Museu Nacional do Azulejo ★★★
Igreja da Madre de Deus
Rua Madre Deus, 4
☎ 21 814 77 47
Tue.-Sat. 10am-5pm
(6pm according to season)
Entry charge.

This museum is housed in a convent founded in 1509 by Queen Dona Leonor. Totally destroyed by the earthquake, it was rebuilt in the Baroque style in the 18th century, but only the church now testifies to the decorative exuberance of the period. Here you can

wander from cloister to cloister, discovering the work of the tile-makers, from the first Moorish-inspired tiles to contemporary azulejos. Don't miss the remarkable panel depicting a panorama of Lisbon before the earthquake, or the story of the hatter Antonio Joaquim Carneiro, which is a bit like a 19th-century comic book. After you've visited the museum, pop into the shop, which offers a good choice of high-quality azulejos (1,800esc each, and around 15,000esc for a handpainted panel). And if all this has given you an appetite, the restaurant situated around the patio is a pleasant place to stop for a drink or a bite to eat.

❷ Mosteiro de São Vicente de Fora ★★
Calçada de S. Vicente
Every day 10am-1pm,
3-5pm, closed Sun.
Entry charge.

You can't miss this large white building with its cupolas that dominate the districts of Graça and the Castelo, but be prepared for a steep climb if you arrive on foot. The first monastery, which was dedicated to St Vincent, dates back to the 12th century and was where the young St Anthony spent his first years as a monk.

The present building was erected on the site in the 16th century. In spite of the successive cloisters lined with blue and white azulejos (representing the *Fables* of La Fontaine and the conquest of Lisbon), you may feel that the monastery is a little empty and austere.

❸ Igreja de Santa Engracia or Panteão Nacional★
Campo de Santa Clara
Tue.-Sun., 10am-5pm
Entry charge.

It took nearly three centuries to complete work on this massive and somewhat unattractive building, hence the popular expression '*obra de Santa Engracia*' ('a Santa Engracia job') which is applied to any task whose completion is postponed indefinitely. The tombs of the some of Portugal's great men, including Prince Henry

the Navigator, Alfonso de Albuquerque and Pedro Alvares Cabral, can be found inside.

❹ Vila Sousa★
Largo da Graça, 82.

❺ Vila Bertha★
Rua do Sol à Graça, 57/59.

In the late 19th century a new type of dwelling appeared in the poorest districts of Lisbon: the multi-family houses, or *habitação economica*, which were the forerunner of present-day council flats. These houses were built between 1880 and 1900, often by the neighbouring industries (particularly the textile mills) to house their workers. The special architecture of these 'villas' was supposed to protect the community from the rest of the city, and aimed to promote mutual aid and solidarity. The Vila Sousa featured a U-shaped building

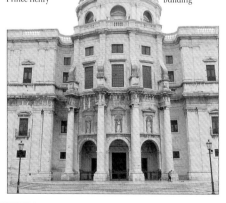

THE LEGEND OF ST VINCENT

Another of Lisbon's legendary saints (along with St Anthony), St Vincent is the patron saint of the city. After being tortured by the Moors, he is said to have run aground in his boat on the shores of the Algarve, before making his way to Lisbon accompanied by two crows, in order to receive a Christian burial. Since then, the crow has been considered as a guardian angel and is an emblem of Lisbon. If you look out for it, you'll see the image of two crows flanking a ship everywhere, engraved in stone or in wrought iron above the streetlights.

constructed round an interior courtyard, while the Vila Bertha boasted a whole village street complete with little houses and private gardens.

❻ Rua da Mouraria★
❼ Rua do Capelão★
❽ Beco do Forno★

Around Rua da Mouraria and Largo Martim Moniz lies the district of Mouraria, which was given to the defeated Arabs in the 13th century by the king, Afonso Henriques, after the conquest of the city. It then became 'their' city, since they were free to practice their religion and trade within its confines. Don't hesitate to take a stroll down its narrow streets, as the district is as picturesque and traditional as the Alfama.

On the banks of the Tagus

The Tagus has always been an integral part of Lisbon life, forming a link between the city and the sea. Recent work to modernise the old port districts has resulted in people rediscovering a taste for the waterfront. The *Rio Tejo* is again taking centre stage, and watching the seagulls and shell fishermen at low tide, taking a *cacilheiro*, climbing the Cristo Rei and dining on the *Outra Banda* (Other Bank) are all part of the Lisbon experience.

❶ Ponte 25 Abril★

Inaugurated in 1966 under Prime Minister Salazar, this suspension bridge was the first to span the Tagus. 3km/ 2 miles long (2km/1 mile of them over the river) and 100m/330ft high, with foundations over 80m/260ft deep, it was an outstanding feat of engineering and was completed in record time (4 years). It links the overcrowded suburbs of the Almada and Cacilhas with the city, and is currently used by over 130,000 vehicles a day, with 45 million crossings a year. On summer Sundays, there are huge traffic jams, when the entire population of Lisbon seems to be returning from the beaches of the Costa de Caparica or the Algarve at the same time.

❷ Ponte Vasco da Gama★★

The new bridge over the Tagus links the eastern part of Lisbon with Montijo, and since it opened in March 1998 it's solved a large part of the traffic problems between the north and south of the country. 18km/11 miles long (10km/5 miles of them over the river), it carries 6 lanes of traffic and cost over 180 million escudos. This cable-stayed bridge with a central span of 420m/1,400ft supported by two 150m/490ft pylons is, along with the Channel Tunnel, one of the greatest engineering projects of the late 20th century.

❸ Cais da Alfândega landing stage and *cacilheiros*★★

Praça do Comercio.

❹ Estação Fluvial de Belém and *cacilheiros*★★

Belém.

Lisbon is above all a port, and life continues to revolve round the *cais* (quays) and *estação fluvial* (landing stages). However, much of the port activity, including fishing,

ship-building, loading and unloading of containers and the docking of oil tankers, stretches for over 30km/18miles upstream or is relegated to the other bank of the river. Morning and evening, the orange and white ferries, or *cacilheiros*, pour a stream of people from the suburbs into the Praça do Comércio. A short crossing between Cais da Alfândega and Cacilhas or between the Estação Fluvial de Belém and Porto Brandão takes around ten minutes and costs under 200esc return.

❺ Cristo Rei★
Almada
Mon.-Sun., 9am-6pm
Entry charge.

This statue, a small replica of Christ the Redeemer in Rio de Janeiro, stands at the mouth of the Tagus.
Erected by Salazar in 1959, it is perched on an 80m/260ft pedestal on top of one of the highest hills

on the left bank of the river. A lift near the statue takes you up to a panoramic terrace, from where there is a fantastic view of the city. Unfortunately, it isn't easy to get here other than by car or taxi.

❻ Atira-te ao Rio★★
Cais do Ginjal, 69/70
Cacilhas/Almada
☎ 21 275 13 80
Closed Mon.

❼ Ponto Final★★
Cais do Ginjal 72
Cacilhas/Almada
☎ 21 23 28 56 or
21 276 07 43
Closed Tue.

If you feel like dining by the waterside, simply take the ferry as far as Cacilhas and then walk for about 10 minutes along the Tagus, with the black waters of the river lapping on your right and the semi-ruined buildings of the old docks to your left. It's worth making the effort to cross to the Outra Banda (Other Bank) and dine with the brilliantly illuminated city laid out before you. The two restaurants are next door to each other, and in the first, **Atira-te ao Rio,** you can dine on exquisite Brazilian food. In the second,

Go with the flow

The best view of Lisbon is the one from the river. It may be unusual to arrive by sea today, but it would be a pity to leave without taking a trip on the Tagus.
TransTej
Estação Fluvial
☎ 21 887 50 58
3,000esc per person
Apr.-Oct. 3pm.

the **Ponto Final**, there's a small but well-chosen menu of traditional Portuguese cuisine. Both restaurants have well-positioned outdoor tables and will offer you *caipirinhas* as an aperitif. Dinner will cost around 7,000–8,000esc for two.

❽ Fragata D. Fernando II and Gloria★★★
Doca de Alcântara
☎ 21 395 20 81
Every day 10am-5pm
Entry charge.

Launched in 1843, this 87m/285ft-long frigate carrying 2,052m²/sqft of sails was the last vessel to sail the India run. It notched up 33 years' service covering over 100,000 nautical miles, and its easy to imagine what life on board was like for the 145 crew members and up to 600 passengers during the three-month crossing. Restored for Expo'98, it makes a fascinating visit.

Parque das Nações, life after Expo '98

The major challenge of the universal exposition of 1998 was the conversion of the industrial district of Xabregas and to make the east of Lisbon a new and attractive urban area. It was a great success, and the Parque das Nações, the ocean-based leisure complex built on the site of Expo '98, continues to flourish.

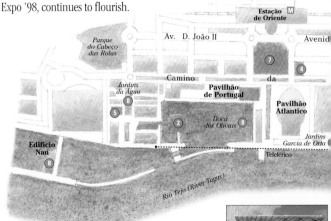

❶ Parque das Nações★★★
☎ 21 891 98 98
📠 21 891 98 21
Sun.-Thu. 9.30am-1am,
Fri.-Sat. 9.30am-3am
Entry free.

The Parque is easily reached from Estação de Oriente, and the best way to start your day is by visiting the main themed pavilions. There's a cable car and little train that

run back and forth between them, but you may prefer to follow the Caminho da Água (Water Way) with its stunning fountains, or stroll in the cool Garcia da Orta gardens.

❷ Oceanarium★★★
☎ 21 891 70 02
Every day 10am-7pm
Entry charge.

This spectacular aquarium is the largest in Europe, and the second largest in the world. A central pool (equivalent in size to four Olympic swimming pools), linked to four side pools illustrate the coastal and underwater ecosystems of the Indian, Pacific, Atlantic and Antarctic Oceans, with over 25,000 fish and animals, including sharks and penguins.

❸ Pavilhão de Macau★★
☎ 21 898 13 10
📠 21 895 54 36
Tue.-Sun. noon-6pm
Entry charge.

The only remaining trace of the Portuguese presence in Macau is the façade of a former church, and behind the replica of it built here lies a reconstruction of the city, with all the mystery of the Orient. The garden is a cool haven and the shop is a delight for those who like tea or Chinese porcelain.

4 Museu Nacional dos Coches★★★

Alameda dos Oceanos
☎ 21 895 59 94
Every day 10am-6pm, closed Tue. Entry charge.

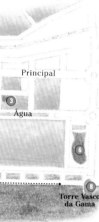

This unique collection of 16th- to 19th-century royal coaches was transferred from Belém to the Parque in May 1999. It includes over 70 vehicles and among the more remarkable exhibits are the wedding carriages of Filipe II and the coach of the papal ambassador.

5 Pavilhão Realidade Virtual★

☎ 21 891 65 44
📠 21 891 65 16
Tue.-Sun. 1-7pm Entry charge.

6 Adrenalina★

Praça Sony
Mon.-Fri. 1-8pm, Sat.-Sun. 11am-8pm. Entry charge.

If you like thrills, then don't miss these two attractions. In the virtual reality (Realidade Virtual)

pavilion, be prepared for a dive in a virtual oceanarium, while at Adrenalina, you can try such exciting activities as trampolining and bungee jumping.

7 Centro Comercial Vasco da Gama★★

Av. D. João II, opposite the Estação de Oriente
☎ 21 895 52 85
Sun.-Thu. 9.30-1am, Fri.-Sat. 9.30-3am Entry free.

Inaugurated in April 1999, this magnificent shopping centre, with 170 shops, 46,000m²/500,000sqft of floor space and an estimated 15 million visitors a year, symbolises the successful regeneration of this part of the city. Expo Urbe, the building project associated with Expo '98, is still going ahead, with 330 hectares/815 acres, including 110 parks, already completed. Homes for twenty-five thousand residents are to be built here and some 18,000 jobs are planned.

8 The restaurant district★★

You can take a tour of the cuisine of the world in the bars and restaurants on the Expo site. For a drink, visit **Peter's Café** (Jardins Garcia da Orta, ☎ 21 895 00 60). If you like meat, try the **Restaurante del Urugay** (Jardins da Agua, ☎ 21 895 54 45) or the Brazilian

EXPO '98, A GREAT SUCCESS

Expo '98 lasted 132 days and brought together exhibits from some 150 countries. Around 10 million people visited the site, of which 21% were foreign visitors. In all, Expo '98 generated well over 6,000 shows and cultural events which were attended by 16.5 million people.

Chimarrão (Olivais, ☎ 21 895 22 22). For Asian food the **Macau** restaurant (Garcia da Orta) or the Korean **Coreia** (Garcia da Orta, ☎ 21 895 57 67) are worth a visit and for gourmet fare, go to **Nobre** (Edifício Nau, ☎ 21 893 46 00) or the **Restaurante Panorâmico Torre** (☎ 21 893 95 50), at the top of the Vasco da Gama tower.

Sintra, the 'Glorious Eden'

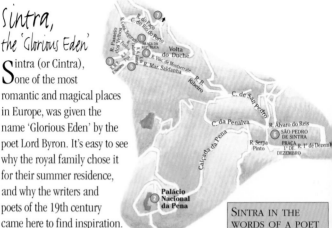

S intra (or Cintra), one of the most romantic and magical places in Europe, was given the name 'Glorious Eden' by the poet Lord Byron. It's easy to see why the royal family chose it for their summer residence, and why the writers and poets of the 19th century came here to find inspiration.

period, and the Pálacio contains one of the most important collections of Spanish-Arabic azulejos in the world. Throughout your visit, you can imagine Luís de Camões reciting *Os Lusíades*, or poor Afonso VI, who was imprisoned in one of the palace bedrooms from 1674 to 1683 having been deposed by his own brother, who seized both his kingdom and his wife.

❶ Palácio Nacional or Palácio Real★★★

Praça da República
☎ 21 923 00 85
Every day 10am-1pm, 2-5pm, closed Wed.
Entry charge.

Every sovereign since King Dom Dinis (1279–1325) has added a wing to this palace, but it was mainly Manuel I who left the mark of his extravagant decorative style. The **Sala das Armas** (Coat of Arms Room) in particular, is lined with azulejo panels depicting hunting scenes and coats of arms of the nobility of the

❷ Palácio Nacional da Pena★★

Parque da Pena
☎ 21 923 02 27
Every day 10am-1pm, 2-5pm (6.30pm in summer)
Entry charge.

Set on a spur of the *serra* in a magnificent park, the Palácio Nacional da Pena is a romantic 19th-century building inspired by the fairy-tale castles of Ludwig II of

Bavaria. The Bavarian prince Ferdinand, husband of Queen Maria II, converted the former monastery into a fanciful, Moorish-inspired palace. You'll be enchanted by the kitsch architecture of the castle and the extraordinary park with its follies, springs and viewpoints overlooking the entire region.

❸ Páteo do Garrett★★
Rua Maria Eugénia F. Navarro, 7
☎ 21 924 33 80,
F 21 924 32 13
Every day 9am-10pm, closed Wed.

This new restaurant is about a ten minute walk up the hill from the centre of town. There's a good view of the chimneys of the Palácio Nacional, as well as attentive service and tasty Portuguese cuisine, especially the *bacalhau a Garett* (salted cod). The food is reasonably priced (which is fairly rare in Sintra) at around 1,500–2,000esc per person.

❹ Pastelaria Piriquita and Piriquita Dois★★★
Rua das Padarias, 1-3
☎ 21 923 06 26
Every day 9am-10pm, closed Wed.

Queijadas, the little cheese and almond tartlets, were a favourite with the kings as long ago as the 12th century, and the Piriquita patisserie is said to have kept the recipe a secret. You can also try

the *travesseiros*, another irresistible Sintra speciality made with cream and almonds. The Piriquita Dois tea room, a little further up the same street, serves the same delicious cakes.

❺ O Patamar★★
Rua da Ferraria, 13
☎ 21 923 57 01
Every day 10am-1pm, 2-7pm.

It's worth climbing the very steep Rua da Ferraria to discover the O Patamar azulejo workshop. The whole production process is carried out by hand and you'll probably be able to see one of the artists at work. The pictures and objects are of high quality, whether they're reproductions of old models or modern designs.

❼ Museu de Arte Moderna, Colecção Berrardo★★★
Av. Heliodoro Salgado
☎ 21 924 81 70

❻ S. PEDRO DE SINTRA★★

The little village of S. Pedro, a few kilometres/ miles from Sintra, is a mecca for antiques and interior decoration. On every other Sunday it hosts a lively **second-hand fair**. If you're lucky enough to be there that day, don't miss the opportunity to go bargain hunting. Otherwise, browse round the many antique and decoration shops:
Alfazema,
Largo 1° de Dezembro, 10,
Banho antigo,
Calçada de S. Pedro, 29,
Real Loja,
Calçada de Penalva,

PRAÇA DA REPÚBLICA

F 21 924 81 77
Wed.-Sun. 10am-6pm
Entry charge.

The 1920s palace that once housed Sintra's casino is now home to the Sintra Museu de Arte Moderna. Thanks to the donation of the Berrardo private collection, it presents a broad retrospective of contemporary art, including works by Picasso, Chiricco, Miró, Pollock, Gilbert and George and Warhol.

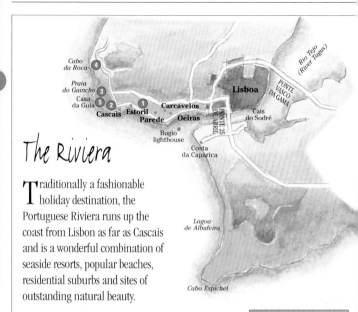

The Riviera

Traditionally a fashionable holiday destination, the Portuguese Riviera runs up the coast from Lisbon as far as Cascais and is a wonderful combination of seaside resorts, popular beaches, residential suburbs and sites of outstanding natural beauty.

❶ Estoril★

Estoril is an elegant resort whose reputation dates back to the 1930s, when it was the favourite high society holiday resort of the day. In the 1940s the crowned heads of Europe, including Umberto II of Italy, Carol II of Romania and the Count of Paris, spent a pleasant exile here. A little later, the Riviera attracted such stars of the silver screen as Rita Hayworth, Orson Wells and Grace Kelly. To this day Estoril is still frequented by members of high society and many aristocratic families and showbiz personalities have villas here and meet regularly on the neighbouring golf courses, at the casino or for the Formula 1 Grand Prix. If you find the idea of an evening in Estoril tempting, you can have dinner at the **Casino** at 8.30pm, followed by a show at 11pm (dinner and show 8,500esc; show only 5,000esc), and the gambling rooms are open until 3am (entry charge 500esc), ☎ 21 468 45 21.

❷ Cascais★★★

The atmosphere of Cascais is completely different to Estoril. Although it's now a major resort, and prominent politicians and wealthy foreigners live here, it's still a working port, as you'll realise by the fishing nets and lobster pots stacked up on the jetty, and a fish market

is held every morning. It's a real pleasure to walk through the narrow streets of the old town, with its charming little squares, houses with fine azulejo façades, magnificent mansions, treasure-filled churches and elegant shops (in Rua Frederico Arouca). End your afternoon with a real Italian ice cream at Santini and have dinner in one of the little restaurants in the Rua das Flores. Here are a few landmarks that will help you find your way around Cascais:

Igreja Nossa Senhora da Assunção, Largo da Assunção. A church with 18th-century azulejos, paintings by Portuguese masters and a painted wooden ceiling.

Santini, Avenida Valbom, 28 ☎ 21 483 37 09.

Palacio Castro Guimarães, Estrada da Boca do Inferno, Tue.-Sun. 10am-5pm. A late 19th-century palace with a large park and a museum.

❸ Cabo da Roca★★

The westernmost point of the European continent is a patch

of desolate heathland that's reminiscent of Cornwall, with windswept gorse and Atlantic rollers breaking on the rocks. In the words of Luís de Camões, it's *'Onde a terra acaba e o mar começa'*, 'where the land ends and the sea begins'. Since 1772 there's only been the lighthouse to show

that man has actually passed this way, and you really feel as if you're standing on the edge of the earth.

❹ Praia do Guincho★★

The wind blows ceaselessly on this beach, forming impressive sand dunes that encroach onto the road. People come from all over the world to surf the rollers of Guincho beach, and it's here that the world wind-surfing championships and many surfing competitions are often held. It's the ideal place to view the roaring Atlantic or take a dip in the ocean (only for the hardy). If you want to have dinner, try **O Mestre Zé** ☎ 21 487 02 75, **O Monte Mar** ☎ 21 486 91 56 or **O Poucaro**.

❺ Casa da Guia ★★★
Quinta São José da Guia, EN 247 Guia 2750 Cascais ☎ 21 486 25 74 Every day 10am-10pm.

The former palace of the counts of Alcáçovas has just been restored, giving you the opportunity to visit this magnificent 19th-century residence. Three floors

of luxury interior decoration shops await you, with many attractive objects for the home. You'll find glass and crystal at Chiaro, household linen at Roupas da Casa and furniture and objects at Cquin. The park boasts a garden centre, restaurant and tea room. In the entrance, **Guia & Brinca** will take care of your children.

> ## OFF TO THE SEASIDE ON BOARD A SUBURBAN TRAIN!
>
> The best way to see the Portuguese Riviera is to travel the 25km/16 miles between Cais do Sodre and Cascais by train. It follows the mouth of the Tagus as far as the ocean, running alongside the water all the way. You'll be able to view the old 17th-century fortifications dotting the coastline and the Bugio lighthouse that divides the estuary in two. The stops in the stations of Oeiras, Carcavelos, Parede and Estoril will allow you a glimpse of the strange mix of seaside resorts and residential suburbs that characterises the coast. **Trains leave Cais do Sodre every 20 mins 5.30am-2.30am.**

Rooms and restaurants
Practicalities

Given the number and variety of places to stay, finding accommodation in Lisbon really isn't a problem. Restaurants that don't look much from the outside often serve the best local cuisine and leave you with the fondest memories.

CHOOSING A HOTEL

There are a number of official categories of accommodation, including:

hotels (rated 2 to 5 stars, plus a *luxo* category), inns, known as **albergaria** or **estalagem** (rated 3 to 4 stars), and **pousada** (charming, luxury hotels in historic locations, somewhat similar to the *paradores* of Spain. Unfortunately, there aren't

any of these in Lisbon itself). There are also **pensão** or **residencial** (guesthouses with a 2 to 4-star rating).

Hotels usually provide a wider range of services than guesthouses, which don't have restaurants (but often provide breakfast and a warmer welcome). There are over 180 hotels and guesthouses in Lisbon and prices are very variable. Generally speaking, you can expect to pay 8,500-15,000esc for a 4-star *pensão-residencial* or 3-star hotel in the city centre, and as much as 20,000-30,000esc for a more luxurious hotel or 4-star *albergaria*.

Prices are generally quoted inclusive of VAT at 17% and include a room and breakfast for two people. They naturally vary according to the season,

and are higher in June, July and August.

Every establishment has a *livro de reclamações*, a book of complaints that they are obliged to hand you if you ask for it. If they don't, you should write to the **Direcção Geral do Tourismo**, Av. Antonio A. de Aguiar, 86, 1004 Lisboa.

RESERVING BEFORE YOU GO

If you don't want to book through a travel agent, you can make a reservation yourself by phone. English is spoken in most hotels. You'll probably be asked to send a fax (or letter) with your credit card number. If you decide to do this, find out the cancellation conditions in advance and ask whether a deposit will be deducted. In any event, if you think you're going to arrive late, confirm your reservation before you leave so they don't give your room to someone else.

FINDING A HOTEL WHEN YOU ARRIVE

It's also perfectly possible to find somewhere to stay when you arrive. Rather than embarking on a hasty random search of the city, get in touch with the tourist information office (see page 8), which will supply you with a list of places to stay and help you make a reservation.

CHOOSING THE BEST DISTRICT TO STAY IN

It's a good idea to choose a central location, if possible in the Lower City (Baixa), if you don't want to keep climbing up and down the very steep streets. You'll easily find a 3-star hotel or guesthouse in the Baixa, and you'll be spoilt for choice between the main international hotels around Avenida da Liberdade . However, there are also charming hotels a little further from the centre (see page 75).

LUNCH OR DINNER

The Portuguese are very fond of good food and fine wine, and there are plenty of restaurants in the city. They're divided into four categories symbolised by forks. Lunch is generally served from 12.30 to 2.30pm, and dinner from 7.30-8pm onwards. Many or the restaurants stop serving at 10.30pm.

Portugaise cuisine is a fairly simple affair based on tasty regional produce, such as olive oil, seafood and fresh vegetables. If you want to try the specialities from the Lisbon area itself, there's *lulas fritas* (fried squid) *iscas* (marinated liver) and, of course, the inevitable *bacalhau* (salted cod), in all its various guises. All the dishes are normally served with potatoes or rice. If you want any other vegetables, you'll need to order them with your main meal. The portions tend to be more generous in restaurants seldom frequented by tourists, and, if you have a small appetite or are not that hungry, it's a common practice to ask for a *meia dose* (half-portion) or share one dish between two. You'll often be served the same dishes in a *tasca* (bistro), *cervejaria* (café) or smart restaurant. It's mainly the decor and service that make a difference to the bill.

HOTELS

Baixa/Avenida da Liberdade

Metrópole★★★ (hotel)

Praça dom Pedro V (Rossio), 30 (Metro Rossio)
☎ 21 346 91 64
📠 21 346 91 66
Double room around 23,000esc.

This recently redecorated hotel, dating from the 1920s, has recovered its former charm. It's remarkably well situated in the heart of the Lower Town and offers some of the best value for money in Lisbon. The rooms, which are all designed differently, are tastefully decorated with antique furniture.

Britânia★★★ (hotel)

Rua Rodrigues Sampaio, 17
☎ 21 315 50 16
📠 21 315 50 21
Double room 20,000–23,000esc.

Tucked away from the hustle and bustle in a street running parallel to Avenida da Liberdade, this hotel has just been entirely redecorated and the lobby has been restored to its former splendour. The marble is gleaming, and the lift flanked by two columns is a fine example of the Art Deco style. The rooms are very large (many also have a sitting room) and attractively furnished. It's a smart, quiet hotel with its own car park.

Veneza★★★ (hotel)

Av. da Liberdade, 189
☎ 21 352 26 18
📠 21 352 66 78
Double room around 18,000esc.

The Veneza offers the charm of a traditional 19th-century hotel, in contrast to some of the bigger chains (Sofitel, Tivoli, etc.) that surround it. Built in 1886 by the lawyer Barata Salgueiro, it's been sympathetically restored to its original style. As you enter, you'll find yourself in a colourful setting, with marvellous frescoes by Pedro Luiz-Gomes. The rooms are well decorated and comfortable, although they can be a little on the small side.

Internacional★★ (hotel)

Rua da Betesga, 3
☎ 21 346 64 01
📠 21 347 86 35
Double room 7,000–16,000esc.

The hotel's Belle Époque façade is difficult to miss, situated as it is on the corner of the Rossio and at the start of Via Augusta. The rooms are vast and clean, although they could do with a little redecoration. It offers an outstanding location at a reasonable price.

Dom Sancho I★★★★ (residencial)

Av. da Liberdade, 202 3rd and 5th floors
☎ 54 86 48
Double room with breakfast 500–10,000esc.

Opposite the luxury hotels of the Avenida, such as the Tivoli and the Sofitel, you'll be surprised to find a pleasant guest house that's incredibly well run with unbeatable prices. The rooms are not only

very well equipped (with en-suite bathroom, television, air conditioning, telephone and mini-bar), they're also quite charming, with typically Portuguese rustic furniture and freshly painted walls. You'll get a warm welcome, and it's probably the *residencial* offering the best value for money in the city, as well as the one with the most central location.

Chiado

Borges★★ (pensão)
Rua Garett, 108
☎ 21 346 19 51
📠 21 342 66 17
Double room
9,500–12,000esc
(depending on season).

This modest establishment's attractions lie in its moderate prices and outstanding location in the heart of the Chiado. It's a little old-fashioned, but the rooms are clean and large.

Belém

Da Torre★★★ (hotel)
Rua dos Jeronimos, 8
☎ 21 363 62 62
📠 21 363 01 61
Double room
14,000–16,000esc.

This is the right place to come if you're hoping to try a piping-hot *pastel de Belém* (cream-filled pastry) for breakfast, or if you want to watch the sunset from the banks of the Tagus. Some rooms even have a view of the Mosteiro dos Jéronimos. The hotel is very cosy and you will immediately feel at home here. The centre of Lisbon isn't all that far away (only 15 minutes by no. 15 tram).

Residencial Setubalense★ (pensão)
Rua de Belém, 28
☎ 21 363 66 39
📠 21 362 13 72
Double room
5,000–8,500esc.

Between the Mosteiro dos Jéronimos and the presidential palace, a fine *azulejo*-covered staircase leads up to this small family guest house. It offers unbeatable prices, incredibly spacious rooms with en-suite bathrooms, and a very warm welcome. In other words, it's a real old-fashioned guest house. It doesn't serve breakfast, but the well-stocked Pastelaria de Belém is nearby.

Fondação Calouste Gulbenkian and the Avenidas

Principe★★★ (hotel)
Av. Duque de Avila, 201
(Metro S. Sebastião)
☎ 21 353 61 51
📠 21 353 43 14
10,000–15,000esc.

A comfortable, modern hotel, just a stone's throw from the Fundação Calouste Gulbenkian and the Parque Eduardo VII. The decor is a little impersonal and somewhat acking in charm, but you'll get a warm welcome and the rooms are relatively spacious.

Amoreiras

Dom Pedro★★★★
Av. Eng. Duarte Pacheco, 24
☎ 21 389 66 00
📠 21 389 66 01
Double room
35,000–50,000esc.

The latest in a line of large Lisbon hotels, Dom Pedro is ideally situated for shopping as it's located near the Centro Comercial das Amoreiras. Refinement and luxury are the order of the day, right down to the smallest detail and there's an amazing view over the whole of Lisbon from the dining room on the top floor.

Bairro Alto

Principe Real★★★★ (residencial)
Rua da Alegria, 53
(Metro Avenida)
☎ 21 346 01 16
📠 21 342 21 04
Double room around
20,000esc.

Located a steep uphill walk from Avenida da Liberdade,

and about 50m/yd from the charming Praça do Príncipe Real, this hotel is well-placed for excursions into the Bairro Alto. The façade is rather dull, but the interior is pleasant and tastefully furnished.

Principe Real-São Bento

Casa de S. Mamede★★★ (pensão)

Rua da Escola Politecnica, 159
☎ 21 396 31 66
🅵 21 395 18 96
Double room
10,500–12,500esc.

This guest house offers a very warm welcome. It's housed in a former palace, but little of its glory remains – just a few azulejos in the lobby and dining room. The rooms are very clean and comfortable, with a slightly old-fashioned charm.

Castelo

Pensão Ninho das Aguias★★

Rua Costa do Castelo, 74
☎ 21 886 70 08
Double room without breakfast 7,000–8,000esc.

This hotel, located on a street that sweeps around the castle, has an amazing view of the city from its terrace. You can have a room with a view but no bathroom, or a room with a bathroom but no view – a difficult decision to make.

Lapa

York House★★★★ (residencial)

Rua das Janelas Verdes, 32 – 1st floor
☎ 21 396 25 44
🅵 21 397 27 93
Double room
22,000–32,500esc.

You can hardly see the entrance of this hotel from the street. The staircase is masked by plants, with only a few azulejos and a discreet porter to show you've come to the right place. Climb

the stairs and you'll arrive in a quiet, romantic courtyard. This former 16th-century convent is now the most charming hotel in Lisbon, with azulejos, marble, old wooden floors, four-poster beds and a patio where it's pleasant to have dinner on a summer evening. Reserve well in advance as the hotel only has 32 rooms and is very popular.

As Janelas Verdes★★★★ (residencial)

Rua das Janelas Verdes, 47
☎ 21 396 81 43
🅵 21 396 81 44
Standard room 28,000esc,
family suite 33,000esc.

This 17-room *residencial* is housed in a lovely 17th-century mansion near the Museu Nacional de Arte Antiga. Once the home of the Portuguese novelist Eça de Queirós, it's easy to believe that the terrace and the azulejos of the patio may have been the source of his inspiration. The rooms are a good size and are tastefully decorated with antique furniture. A family-run concern, you'll get the pleasant impression of staying in a private home. Book in advance

Hotel da Lapa★★★★★

Rua Pau de Bandiera, 4
☎ 21 395 00 05
🅵 21 395 06 65
Double room 35,000esc
(47,000esc in June).

A sumptuous five-star hotel, with an open-air swimming pool and an amazing view of the Tagus. The atmosphere is typical of the Lapa district, where discreet luxury hides behind the pink and ochre façades of the magnificent mansions and palaces.

Estoril coast. It's definitely one of the most charming hotels in the Lisbon area and is the ideal place for a special weekend.

Nossa Senhora da Guia★★★★ (estalagem)

Estrada do Guincho (Cascais)
☎ 21 486 92 39
ℱ 21 486 92 27
Double room with sea view 25,000esc, without view 20,000esc.

If you like the and the sound of the waves, then this *estalagem* is for you. It overlooks the magnificent Guincho beach, whose famous Atlantic Ocean rollers are a magnet for surfers and windsurfers alike. Situated on the very edge of the European continent, it's far from the noise and fumes of the city. Antique furniture and excellent service will take you back to another era, and you may even forget about Lisbon altogether. You will need a car as it's around 25km/16 miles from the centre of Lisbon.

Graça

Albergaria Senhora do Monte ★★★★ (residencial)

Calçada do Monte, 39
☎ 21 886 60 02
ℱ 21 887 77 83
Double room 17,000esc, with terrace 27,500esc.

This modern hotel is a bit of a climb if you're on foot, but you'll be glad you made the effort when you see the marvellous view of Lisbon that it commands. Its location is really one of the main attractions of this slightly out-of-the-way *residencial*, so make sure that you ask for a room with a view. The rooms were redecorated recently and are comfortable, though a little lacking in character.

Cascais

Albatroz★★★★★ (hotel)

Rua Frederico Arouca, 100 (Cascais)
☎ 21 483 28 21
ℱ 21 484 48 27
Double room with sea view 42,000esc, without view 35,000esc.

The former palace of the Duques de Loulé, better known as the 'Caixinha de Amêndoas', has been turned into a luxury hotel without losing any of its 19th-century style. The bar and some of the rooms have an unforgettable view of the sea and the

Sintra

Casa da Tapada★★★ (tourismo de habitação)

Tapada das Roças
☎ 21 923 03 42
Double room around 22,500esc.

This charming family pension, listed as a *'tourismo de habitação',* is midway between a guest house and a hotel and offers a warm welcome in the peaceful setting of the forest of Sintra. With five suites, a garden and a swimming pool, it's ideal for nature lovers and romantics alike. You'll have to hire a car if you want to visit Lisbon.

RESTAURANTS

Docas/Alcântara

Salsa Latina★★★

Gara Maritima d'Alcântara
☎ 21 395 05 50.

This restaurant, housed in the right wing of the Gara Maritima d'Alcântara, has a vast terrace overlooking the Tagus and is the ideal place for a romantic dinner. The contemporary interior has been tastefully designed and you won't be disappointed by the cuisine either. Try the *lulas* (squid) *a la Sevillana* and *peixe a la madeirense* (Madeira-style fish with bananas). Leave a little room for some cheese and ask for *queijo da Serra amanteigado* (ripe ewe's cheese), which should be eaten the Portuguese way, with a teaspoon and accompanied by grapes. After midnight, the mood changes and everyone takes to the dance floor, with salsa lessons and concerts every evening.

Doca Seis★★

Doca de Santo Amaro, Armazém 6
☎ 21 395 79 05
🅕 21 395 78 94.

Make your way to the first floor and try to get a round table in the bay window so that you can feast your eyes on the luxurious marina below. You'll appreciate the cuisine that includes home-made *bacalhau*

(salted cod) and shrimp gratin. If you can't make up your mind what to have, the *gambas* (prawns) are a good bet. Children are always made to feel welcome here, which makes this an ideal restaurant for a family meal.

Zeno★★

Doca de Santo Amaro
☎ 21 397 39 51.

A converted warehouse situated on the river, Zeno is always busy, whatever time of day you visit. At the end of the working day, people come here straight from the office for an aperitif, and if you want to have dinner, it's essential to book in advance. After 11pm it gets so busy that it's difficult to even get a drink at the bar, let alone find a seat in the attic room to listen to the live music. Perhaps its success is due to the warm, Baroque decor of bright yellow walls, old wooden doors and fabulous chandeliers, the tasty Brazilian cuisine or even the charming waitresses, but this popular, lively restaurant has become *the* place to see and be seen in Lisbon, so make sure you include a visit to it in your plans.

Indochina★★

Rua da Cintura do Porto de Lisboa, Armazém H Rocha Conde de Obidos
☎ 21 395 58 75.

It's a good idea to book in advance as Indochina is one of the latest restaurants to open in the district and is very

popular. It's already a regular meeting-place for Lisbon's trendy yuppies, who all get together here on Saturday nights. The dishes aren't typically Indo-Chinese, but they're subtly flavoured and extremely delicious.

Blues Café★★

Rua da Cintura do Porto de Lisboa, Armazém H Rocha Conde de Obidos
☎ 21 395 70 85.

You have to come here after dark to fully appreciate the atmosphere generated by the light filtering through the voluminous red velvet drapes and the warm wooden decor. It's as if you've been suddenly transported to a New Orleans bar. One of the owners, Reiner Kuipers, a Dutchman who has made Lisbon his home, claims that he got the inspiration for the decor from his travels in Lousiana and South Africa. Cajun and international cuisine are served from 8pm to 1am, with blues playing in the background and a jazz concert at 11pm once a week.

Alcântara Café★★★

Rua Maria Luisa Holstein, 15 (Rua da Cozinha Economica)
☎ 21 363 71 76.

The Alcântara Café is the mecca of Lisbon nightlife and is always busy. Choose your outfit carefully, though, as this is one of the most fashionable nightspots in Lisbon and the competition's fierce. The cuisine is French-inspired, but you won't find it easy to concentrate on your food because of everything that's going on around you. The Alcântara has an amazing decor, with gigantic columns, a metal ceiling, impressive hangings, a huge number of mirrors and bronze Rodin-style sculptures, not to mention the novel bar and toilets. Many of the regular clients come here for dinner before continuing their evening at the neighbouring disco, the Alcântara Mar, which is the city's trendiest club of the moment, and is open until late so you can party Lisbon-style.

Doca Jardim do Marisco

Jardim do Marisco★★

Av. Infante D. Henrique Jardim do Tabacco
☎ 21 882 42 42.

In a very short space of time, the last of the remaining docks (the Jardim do Tabacco) opposite Santa Apolónia station has become the fashionable place to begin and end the evening. You can dine opposite the Tagus at the Jardim do Marisco, which is owned by the famous Portuguese actor, Herman José. This trendy restaurant is always busy at the weekend, so book in advance if you want a table for dinner.

Cintura do Porto de Lisboa

Porcão

Rua da Cintura do Porto de Lisboa, 79 Armazém 7
☎ 21 395 06 46
Mon.-Sat. 12.30-3.30pm, 8pm-1am, Sun. closed 11.30pm.

Soon there won't be anything left of the old traditional port of Lisbon, as the last remaining docks have been renovated. All the warehouses along the railway and Avenida 24 de Julho have now been converted into restaurants or discos, and of all of them, Porcão is the place not to miss. The space is put to very good use, with an interior colour scheme and furniture that give the impression of being in a South American hacienda. There's an appetising buffet where you can eat as much as you like, as well as enjoying an excellent selection of freshly grilled meats, and all for a very reasonable 3,500esc per person.

Principe Real/São Bento/Estrêla

Comida de Santo★

Calçada Miguel Pàis, 39
☎ 21 396 33 39.

This Brazilian restaurant is small and intimate, and is an ideal place for dinner for two. Even if you haven't got anything in particular to celebrate, start with a house *caipirinha* and some delicious *pãozinhos de queijo* (small cheesecakes that are served warm). Enjoy a tasty

meal and a couple of cocktails in this busy restaurant, an ideal place to start the evening.

Conventual★★★

Praça das Flores, 45
☎ 21 390 91 96.

Located in the most charming square in Lisbon, this former

convent has been converted into a restaurant, with a monastic decor, creative cuisine, an impressive wine list and heavenly desserts – what more could you want? The Conventual is one of the best restaurants in Lisbon and the food is always of the highest standard.

Umpuntocinco★★

Rua Marcos Portugal, 1/5 (Praça das Flores)
☎ 21 396 48 95
Ⓕ 21 60 56 37.

In case the monastic style of the Conventual isn't to your liking, you'll find the Umpuntocinco, another high-quality restaurant, in the same romantic little square. It has a soothing decor, with salmon pink walls, green-painted chairs covered with pretty fabric and matching Alcobaça tableware (don't trouble to ask where you can buy some – it was made to order for the restaurant). Try the house-speciality, *bife punto cinco*, (beef stuffed with cheese and baked in the oven), and wash it down with a Luis Pato tinto in a large burgundy-style wine glass. A classy restaurant, but quite pricey.

XL★

Calçada da Estrêla, 57 A 63
☎ 21 395 61 18.

The name of this restaurant is pronounced 'sheeshel'. It's the Portuguese Parliament's favourite brasserie, and you can have fun trying to spot ministers and other prominent politicians while you eat your meal. Some people say the house speciality, the XL steak, is not as good as it once was, but it's very tasty and you still get an excellent assortment of *molhos* (sauces). If you've got an especially big appetite, however, don't expect XL portions!

Templo dos Sabores★

Travessa do Conde de Soure, 15A
☎ 21 346 35 00
Mon.-Sat. 12.30-3.30pm, 8-11.30pm, closed Sat. lunchtime.

It was a bold move to build a new 'temple of flavours' in the heart of the São Bento district. The decor makes an inviting setting for the creative cuisine, while the discreet, attentive service leaves you totally free to appreciate it.

Bairro Alto

Sinal Vermelho★

Rua das Gaveias, 89
☎ 21 346 12 52
Ⓕ 21 343 12 81.

Stop at the 'Red Light' (*Sinal Vermelho*) but be prepared to queue if you haven't booked

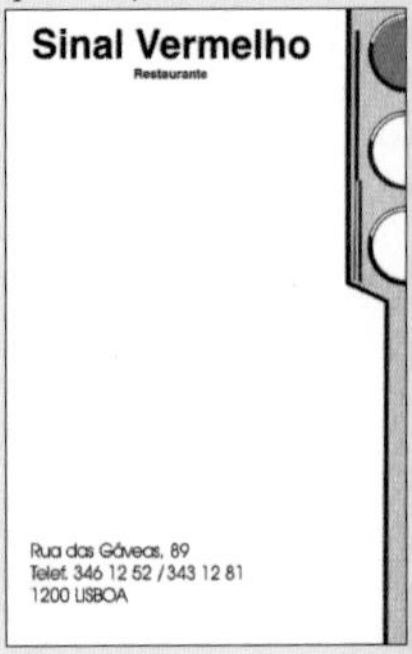

in advance. Don't waste time looking at the menu, follow the locals' example and order the house speciality, *açorda de mariscos* or *açorda de bacalhau*. It's a bread soup made from garlic or onions, eggs, coriander and seafood or salted fish, that's baked in the oven. A popular restaurant with a great atmosphere and good, traditional food.

Massima Culpa★

Rua da Atalaia, 35-37
☎ 21 342 01 21
Thu.-Sun. 7pm-2am.

According to the Italian residents of Lisbon, this is the best restaurant in the city for pasta or risotto. The Milanese chef has forgotten none of the secrets of Italian home cooking, and he produces exquisite, traditional Mediterranean food. Popular with families, it's one of the few restaurants in Lisbon that stays open until 2am on Sundays.

Chiado

Tágide★★★

Largo da Academia Nacional de Belas Artes, 18 and 20
☎ 21 342 07 20.

Tagide has a marvellous view of the Castelo and the Tagus and an imposing decor, with azulejos from an Alentéjo *quinta* and spotless white linen tablecloths. It may be costly and a little formal, but both the food and the service are excellent. Book a table for a big night out, but make sure you dress up for the occasion, otherwise you may feel out of place. It's a very traditional and stylish restaurant with accordingly high prices.

Amoreiras/Rato

Casa da Comida★★★

Travessa das Amoreiras, 1
☎ 21 388 53 76
☎ 21 387 51 32.

This is the chic canteen for Portuguese and foreign businessmen, and sombre suits, shirts and ties are the order of the day. The slightly old-fashioned but classic decor includes Chinese porcelain, and Old Masters, but the tables are dispersed around a charming garden, ensuring a modicum of privacy. If you want to rub shoulders with Lisbon society, if only for an evening, then this is the place to come for a stylish, if expensive, meal.

Baixa/Av. da Liberdade

Solar do Presunto★★

Rua das Portas de Sto. Antão, 150
☎ 21 342 42 53
☎ 21 346 84 68.

If you're in Lisbon between February and April and you want to experience some new flavours, don't miss the speciality of this restaurant, *lampreia* (lamprey). Part-fish and part-snake, this creature has travelled a long way, since it crosses the Atlantic to lay its eggs in the estuaries of northern Portugal. This is a fatal error, as it lands up on the tables of the best restaurants in Lisbon and Porto. The usual way to cook it is marinated in its own blood, together with red wine and herbs, then it's served with rice. You can see it before it's cooked if you want, but it's probably better to avoid this if you're squeamish.

Os Tibetanos★

Rua do Salitre, 117
☎ 21 314 20 38
☎ 21 352 40 76.

Situated in the Buddhist Centre, this is an inspired setting for a lunch break. On a fine day, you can sit down to vegetable curry, tofu or vegetarian tart while sipping carrot juice on the terrace. Bordering the magnificent Jardim d'Alegria, where coloured flags painted with Buddhist mantras wave in the breeze, the city seems a long way away. The place has an authentic Tibetan feel, and you can experience the peace of the Zen meditation centre.

Casa do Alentejo★★

Rua das Portas de Sto. Antão, 58
☎ 21 346 92 31.

Os Tibetanos
Restaurante
Salão de Chá

Rua do Salitre 117 - 1250 LISBOA   Tel. 214 20 38 Fax 352 40 76
FECHADO DOMINGOS E FERIADOS

A little corner of Alentéjo in the heart of Lisbon, this late 19th-century Moorish-style palace is the meeting-place of all those who are homesick for the region. Its magnificent patio offers food and a setting typical of Alentéjo, and its vast, slightly old-fashioned sitting rooms are the scene of family reminiscences. You can try specialities, such as spare ribs of pork and *cataplana a l'alentejana* (stewed fish or meat), in the large azulejo-lined rooms and watch a folk dancing on Saturday evenings.

Belém

T-Clube★★★

Av. Brasilia
Edificio Espelho d'Agua
☎ **21 301 66 52**
🖷 **21 301 58 81.**

The *T-Clube* is a restaurant, bar and nightclub rolled into one, and is one of the trendiest places in Lisbon. In an amazing high-tech setting on the banks of the Tagus, you can enjoy French-style cuisine as well as good, traditional Portuguese specialities, such as the celebrated *arroz de pato* (duck with rice). After 11pm, head for the bar where you can enjoy a drink while you wait for the evening's spectacular firework display to begin.

A lively and varied selection of music is played, which will encourage you to dance the night away on the busy dance floor.

Castelo/Alfama

Arco do Castelo★

Rua Chão da Feira, 25
☎ **21 887 65 98**
Mon.-Sat. noon-midnight, closed Sun.

It's hard to pass by the exotic smells that waft from the kitchen of this charming little restaurant at the foot of the Castelo walls. With just ten simple tables adorned with checked tablecloths, and a warm welcome from Pedro, you'll immediately feel at home. Try the prawn or chicken *caril* (curry), the crab *xeque-xeque* or the *feijoada indiana* (Indian sausages). Ask for your food to be either *meio piquante*, slightly spicy, or *piquante*, if you like your food very hot. Remember to leave some room for the delicious creamy ice cream (*nata*) with mango coulis, which is cooling to the palate after your hot meal. The restaurant also offers an excellent choice of Portuguese wines. Make sure you book, as it's often full, and expect to pay 5,000–6,000esc for two.

O Bacalhau de Molho★★

Beco dos Armazéms de Lisboa, 1
☎ **21 886 37 67.**

If you want to try every conceivable way that *bacalhau* (salted cod) can be prepared, it may be difficult in a weekend, but O Bacalhau de Molho will at least give you an idea of the variety available. You'll find every kind of *bacalhau* dish here – *a bràs* (with eggs, onions and potatoes), *espiritual* (with carrots), *tropical* (with pineapple), *com natas* (with cream), and *com espinafres* (with spinach). Ask for a *meia dose* (half-portion), and try a bit of everything that you fancy.

A Tasquinha★

Largo do Contador Mor, 5–7
☎ **21 887 68 99**
Closed Sun.

You can enjoy a rest in the shade of this charming little square when you stop for a break at the Tasquinha. It's one of those typical bistros that continue to offer good, simple, authentic Portuguese cuisine. Find a seat on the terrace and ask for the grilled sardines or the squid.

Olimpio

Rua Santa Cruz do Castelo, 82
☎ **21 888 26 46**
Tue.-Sat. 8pm-1am.

Although this narrow street in the Santa Cruz district looks rather seedy after dark, don't be deceived by appearances as it's really quite safe. Olivier, the young chef of the Olimpio, is the son of the famous Portuguese restauranteur, Michel, and his cuisine is totally authentic. The *carpaccio* is delicious, as are the little black puddings. Make sure you follow the chef's recommendations and you certainly won't be disappointed.

Lapa

York House★★★
Rua das Janelas Verdes, 32
☎ 21 396 25 44.

If it's your wedding anniversary and you're planning a special candlelit dinner for two, York House is the ideal place to come. In summer you can dine under the palm trees in the delightful courtyard or, if there's a chill in the air, in one of the cosy little rooms lined with blue and white azulejos. You can relax far from the hustle and bustle of the city and you'll find yourself whispering so as not to disturb the serene setting. They serve good, classic cuisine, including vegetarian options, and all at reasonable prices.

Picanha★★
Rua das Janelas Verdes, 96
☎ 21 397 54 01.

This very pleasant Brazilian restaurant is housed in the entrance hall of a former 18th-century palace, as testified by the imposing arch of the door and the blue and white azulejos. It can be very difficult to get a table here and it's best to book well in advance. Once you're in, sit back and relax as you can have as much as you like of the house speciality, which is the only dish on the menu. The dish in question is *picanha*, a delicious beef

marinated in a subtle mixture of spices, then grilled and served rare, accompanied by red beans, salad, rice and the inevitable *farofa* (toasted cassava). Don't forget to say 'stop' when you've had enough, otherwise they'll carry on serving you. Expect to pay 1,950esc per person for the *picanha* only – anything else is extra. This restaurant doesn't take credit cards.

Nariz do Vinho Tinto★★
Rua do Conde, 75
☎ 21 395 30 35
Every day noon-3pm, 7pm-midnight.

Literally translated, the name of the restaurant means 'Red Wine Nose'. It's a characterful place with a style of its own. There's nothing fancy about the decor or service, but you feel really at home here, and it is very popular with the locals. All the food is freshly cooked, which means you could be in for a bit of a wait. Try the *arroz de pato* (duck with rice) or the *açorda de mariscos* (bread soup with seafood). The smells wafting from the traditional cast-iron cooking-pots that are placed on the tables aren't deceptive, as everything is absolutely delicious here. It's essential to book at the weekend.

The coast of Lisbon

A Pastorinha★★★
Avenida Marginal
Praia de Carcavelos
(Carcavelos)
☎ 21 458 04 92
❶ 21 458 05 32.

A Pastorinha has a prime location, and before you lies nothing but the ocean, rolling away endlessly to the horizon. The friendly owner of the restaurant will greet you personally, and if you engage him in conversation he'll proudly reel off the names of the famous people who have dined in his restaurant. They include no fewer than two presidents of the Republic and at least a dozen ministers of state. One thing you can be sure of is that you'll eat the best seafood *cataplana* (casserole) or *parillada* (grills) in Lisbon here, and the prawns are just out of this world.

CAFÉS, TEAROOMS AND ICE CREAM PARLOURS

Baixa/Chiado

Bénard★★

Rua Garett, 104
☎ 21 347 31 33

Mon.-Sat. 8am-midnight, closed Sun.

This traditional café is the ideal place to stop for a break from an afternoon's shopping, and you can sit either on the terrace or in the dining-room. If you'd rather carry on window shopping, buy a delicious croissant to take away. Choose one with a jam or cream filling (vanilla, chocolate, etc.) if you feel like something sweet, or ham and cheese if you'd rather have something savoury. At Easter, you can try the local speciality, a kind of brioche crown with a hard-boiled egg in the middle.

Caffè Rosso★★

Rua Garett, 19
Loja D
☎ 21 347 15 24.

You have to pass under a porch in the Rua Garett to find this bar and tearoom, housed in a charming courtyard in the

café bar
CAFFÈ ROSS
Rua Garett, 19, Loja D - 1200 LISBOA
PORTUGAL

Chiado. The surrounding buildings have just been renovated, and there are some good shops in the area. The place is popular with the local business people and you often have to wait to get a seat under the big white parasols on the terrace. It's worth it, though, as the interior is a little grim. There are the usual sandwiches and salads on the menu, but if you've got a good appetite you may find the portions rather small.

Sao Bento/Estrela

Pastelaria 1800

Largo do Rato, 7

Mon.-Sat. 6am-10pm, closed Sun.

As the beautiful multi-coloured *azulejo* panels at the back of the room depict, they've been making cakes in this patisserie since 1857. Do as the Portuguese do and have a *gallão* (coffee) and a *bollo de Arroz* (rice cake) standing at the bar.

Amoreiras

A Veneziana

Centre Comercial Amoreiras
Av. Duarte Pacheco
Loja 3019
☎ 21 383 21 72
Every day 10am-midnight

In 1933 a family of Italians from the north of the country moved to Lisbon and opened the city's first ice cream parlour in Avenida da Berna. It was an immediate success, and they had to make deliveries to every district to satisfy demand. The parlour in Avenida da

Berna has now gone, but Italian ice cream is still made the traditional way in the Centro Comercial das Amoreiras.

Lapa

Chà da Lapa★★

Rua do Olival, 8
☎ **21 60 08 88**
Every day 9am-8pm.

A real tearoom with a cosy, deliciously British atmosphere,

featuring plush red velvet seats, soft lighting and trompe-l'œil decoration. Everything here is homemade. The cakes and petits fours are delicious, and at lunchtime you can fill up on a hot meal, a mixed salad or a savoury tart. washed down with a cup of *chà*, of course.

Dom Garfo★

Rua da Lapa, 36
☎ **21 395 09 40**
Mon.-Sat. 9am-8pm,
closed Sun.

From the outside, you can get the impression that this is an interior design shop selling kitchen utensils, spice jars, trays, carafes and multi-coloured bottle stoppers. Inside, it's an altogether different scene, with painted wooden tables and chairs, and a very

rustic atmosphere. The menu includes savoury *pasteis* (pastries) of every kind, one or two regional dishes of the day and some delicious creamy desserts.

Avenidas

A Mexicana

Av. Guerra Junqueiro, 30 C
☎ **21 848 61 17**
Every day 8am-midnight

This is the meeting-place of Lisbon's fashionable and wealthy. Sit on the terrace and watch as they show off their new cars or latest *telemoveis* (mobile phones). The ice creams are all homemade and absolutely delicious. If you're keen on chocolate, try the *Donatella* (a smooth mixture of chocolate, hazelnut and vanilla) or the *Mexicana*

(the Portuguese version of *stracciatella* – vanilla ice cream with chocolate chips).

Say it with words

Ordering tea or coffee can sometimes be a little complicated. You really have to know what you want.

■ *Um Italiano* is a very strong Italian-style espresso.
■ *Uma bica* is a fairly strong espresso.
■ *Um pingado* is a 'hazelnut' (an espresso with a dash of milk).
■ *Um galão* is a white coffee (with more milk than coffee) served in a tall glass.
■ *Uma meia de leite* or *um café com leite* is a large cup of white coffee.
■ *Uma carrioca de café* is coffee diluted with water.
■ *Um chà* is tea (*com leite* – with milk, *com limão* – with lemon).
■ *Uma carrioca de limão* is hot lemon juice.

Shopping
Practicalities

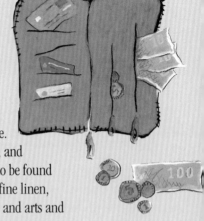

Even if you haven't come to Lisbon with the intention of shopping, you're in for a nice surprise. The city has plenty to offer, and some of the best bargains to be found are the handmade goods (fine linen, leather goods, azulejo tiles and arts and crafts of every kind).

WHERE TO SHOP

The shopping districts are relatively concentrated in Lisbon. If you're in a hurry, you'll find everything you need in the Baixa or the Chiado. If you like to buy things for the home and trinkets, try the Campo de Ourique. If you're keen on bargain-hunting, the secondhand shops of the Príncipe Real and S. Bento districts will keep you busy. If you're a Sunday shopper, you can go straight to one of the big shopping centres of Lisbon (Amoreiras or Vasco de Gama) or the surrounding area (Colombo, Oeiras or Cascais).

FINDING YOUR WAY

Next to each address in the Shopping and Nightlife sections we have shown its location on the map of Lisbon located on pages 84-85.

OPENING HOURS

The shops are generally open Monday to Friday from 9am (or 9.30am) to 1pm (or 1.30pm) and 3pm (or 3.30pm) to 7pm. They normally close at 1pm on Saturdays, except in December, when they stay open in the afternoon for Christmas shoppers. In the shopping and tourist districts (the Chiado and Belém), some shops open on Saturday afternoons, whereas in the Baixa, you'll find most of them are shut.

WEEKEND SHOPPING

The supermarkets stay open all day Saturday (**Pingo Doce**, **Pão d'Açucar**, etc.). Some (**Loja Select**) are even open 365 days a year from 7am to 2am. The shopping centres stay open all weekend from 9am to midnight. This is true of **Amoreiras** (Rua Eng. Pacheco Duarte ☎ 21 381 02 00), the new Vasco de Gama shopping centre (see page 64), the Colombo centre (see page 113) and **Cascais Shopping** (Est. Nacional 9, Alcabideche ☎ 21 460 06 46). Here you'll find not only small shops selling clothes, shoes and objects for the home, but also large food shops. In the **Centro Cultural de Belém**, some shops open on Saturday afternoons and Sundays.

Secondhand markets are held on Sundays on the coast between Lisbon and Cascais (alternating with Alges, Paço do Arcos, Oeiras and Cascais), at São Pedro de Sintra depending on the Sunday in the month and, since 1999, in the Parque das Nações on the second and third Sunday in the month (see page 64).

PAYING FOR YOUR GOODS

Most shops take international credit cards. If they don't, it's better to withdraw money from one of the many cash machines throughout the city and pay in cash. A hefty commission is charged on traveller's cheques and foreign currency.

Every time you pay, the shopkeeper must give you a receipt, which you should keep in a safe place. In general, this purchase invoice is indispensable. You may be asked to produce it when you go through customs, and it will be useful if you ever wish to sell your purchase or need to complete a claim form if you're unlucky enough to be burgled. Always ask for an invoice as well as a certificate of authenticity when buying a work of art or piece of antique furniture.

CUSTOMS

Duty free allowances between EU countries were abolished in 1999 so there are no limits to what you can bring in and out of the country if you are travelling from a member country, and so long as it is for personal use. Duty free allowances for non-EU

citizens are limited to 200 cigarettes; 50 cigars; 1 litre spirits or 2 litres of wine or beer; 50g perfume; 500g coffee and 100g tea.

TRANSPORTING BULKY OBJECTS

If you're afraid of breaking your beautiful azulejo tile panel or the precious porcelain dinner service you couldn't resist, ask the shop where you bought them whether they can ship them home for you. You can also go along to the post office yourself and use the packaging that's available especially for the purpose. The cost of sending the goods will depend on their weight. However, there are no guarantees for anything very fragile and the volume that can be sent is fairly limited. For bulkier objects and furniture, you'll need to call in a specialised transportation company.

TNT Express Worldwide
☎ 21 848 41 31
For azulejo tiles and crockery only, by plane (24hrs, 16,000esc for 5kg/11 lb) or lorry (1 week, 23,000esc for 11-25kg/24-55lb), insurance costs extra. They will come to collect the objects themselves.

Transportes Galamas
☎ 21 444 30 21
For furniture and works of art. They take care of packing and insurance and give quotations by appointment (they will visit the shop for an estimate if necessary).

Danzas
☎ 21 230 70 00
This well-known firm has a subsidiary in Portugal that you can contact direct.

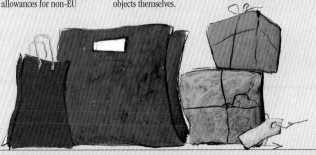

WOMEN'S FASHION

Over the past few years, a new generation of Portuguese designers has appeared on the scene, with flourishing workshops in the Bairro Alto and Chiado. Alongside already well-known names, such as Ana Salazar, Fátima Lopes and José Carlos, other talented designers are emerging, including José Antonio Tenente, Nuno Gama, Manuel Alves and José Manuel Gonçalves. Others who are still relatively unknown, such as João Tomé, Francisco Pontes, Dino Alves and Lena Aires, produce attractive one-off designs and made-to-measure garments

STYLISTS AND DESIGNERS

Ana Salazar

Rua do Carmo, 87 (C3)
Baixa
☎ 21 347 22 89
Av. de Roma, 16E (D1)
Avenidas
☎ 21 848 67 99
Mon.-Fri. 10am-7pm, Sat. 10am-1pm.

Ana Salazar is well-respected in the fashion industry and is certainly the best-known fashion designer in Portugal. Her designs are made from leather and shiny, synthetic materials in neutral shades of black, grey, brown, navy and white. Featuring long, enveloping shapes, it's a distinctive look that you'll either love or hate.

Gardenia

Rua Nova do Almada, 94/96/98/100 (C3)
Chiado
☎ 21 347 20 26
Mon.- Sat. 10am-7pm.

A vast shop that's immaculately presented in a newly renovated building in the Chiado. The clothes are beautifully arranged in separate areas to make it easy for you to find your way through the designer jungle. Nuno Gama and Fátima Lopes feature among a number of Portuguese and foreign designers whose clothes are on sale here.

Fátima Lopes

Avenida de Roma, 44 D/E
Avenidas (D1)
☎ 21 849 59 86
Mon.-Fri. 10.30am-7.30pm, Sat. 10.30am-1pm, 2-7.30pm
Rua da Atalia, 6 (C3)
☎ 21 324 05 78
Mon.-Sat. 11am-7pm.

Fátima Lopes belongs to the new

generation of fashion designers who've already made their mark in the industry. She sees fashion as a way of communicating with others, and her daring, figure-hugging clothes combine geometrical appliqué with vivid, graphic colours (blood red, electric blue and black and white). She makes good use of the latest avant-garde materials, such as lycra lace, polyamide jersey and matt leatherette. She has recently introduced a sensual and daring lingerie collection to her range.

Manuel Alves and José Manuel Gonçalves

**Hotel Dom Pedro, Av. Eng.
Duarte Pacheco, 24 (B2)**

☎ 21 347 51 37
Mon.-Fri. 1-8pm,
Sat. 11am-4pm.

This well-known and shocking pair of Portuguese fashion designers have abandoned the Bairro Alto in favour of the lobby of the very smart *Hotel Dom Pedro*. As always, drapes, asymmetry and a touch of the exotic — mandarin collars and Oriental silks — make for sophisticated, exquisite and feminine clothes. A classy shop, but with prices to match.

José Carlos

**Travessa do Monte
do Carmo, 2
Chiado (C3)
☎ 21 347 25 47
Mon.-Sat. 11am-8pm.**

José Carlos's designer clothes are surprisingly varied, and this is the ideal shop to find clothes to suit every aspect of your modern lifestyle. For the slick businesswoman there are beautiful tailored jackets, tops with provocative necklines and body-hugging leather skirts. For the evening there are beautiful dresses inspired by the mystery of the Orient, or, for the more daring, there are long semi-transparent muslin sheath dresses that will show off your figure and make you the talk of the town as you dance the night away in Lisbon's clubs and discos.

José Antonio Tenente

**Travessa do Carmo, 8
Chiado (C3)
☎ 21 342 25 60
Mon.-Sat. 10.30am-7.30pm.**

José Antonio Tenente was the designer chosen to convey the image of Portuguese fashion during Expo '98, and he designed the blue and yellow uniforms (the colours of the logo) for the staff. However, you'll find his normal collections in his shop in the Chiado, including well-cut silk, cotton or wool jackets in good, strong colours — clothes that look as if they were made for you and that you'll want to wear right away.

Loja Branca

**Praça das Flores, 48A
S. Bento (B3)
☎ 21 60 90 28
Mon.-Fri. 2-8pm.**

Manuela Gonçalves designs a unique collection of clothes for women. A few minutes' walk from the designers of the Bairro Alto, her shop in Praça das

Cristina Lopes
Rua do Carmo, 31 loja 6
Chiado (C3)
☎ **21 343 21 43**
Every day 10am-7.30pm.

This shop stocks just a small number of styles – and each in one size only – a few well-cut dresses, jackets and skirts made of fine fabrics. Don't worry if you can't find what you're looking for in the collection on display, they'll make the clothes to your size in the fabric of your choice

Flores is a delight, filled with really attractive, wearable clothes in natural fabrics. The shapes are original, while remaining simple and elegant. It's probably quite fortunate that she doesn't take credit cards, otherwise you might be tempted to spend more than you intended.

Lena Aires
Rua da Atalaia, 96
Bairro Alto (C3)
☎ **21 346 18 15**
Every day 2-6pm,
closed Sun.

If you want to get an idea of the creativity of the new wave of Portuguese designers, come and visit the wild, psychedelic world of Lena Aires. Here you'll find an unusual range of clothes in a bold mixture of fabrics and colours.

(a jacket costs 20,000esc and a skirt costs 7,000esc). Unfortunately it takes two weeks and you have to pay for delivery.

WOMEN'S SIZES
Bras and bodies

UK sizes					
30	32	34	36	38	40

Portuguese sizes					
36	38	40	42	44	46

Clothes

UK sizes						
8	10	12	14	16	18	20

Portuguese sizes						
34	36	38	40	42	44	46

HIGH STREET FASHION

Naturel pour femme

**Rua da Prata, 211
Baixa (C3)
☎ 21 382 56 05
Rua Ferreira
Borges, 121A
Campo de
Ourique (B2)
☎ 21 386
53 13
Every day
10am-7pm.**

Take no notice
of the shop's
French name,
since Naturel pour
femme belongs
to a Portuguese
ready-to-wear
manufacturer.
The clothes are
feminine, easy to wear,
and are produced
in a range of
natural colours.
The prices are
also very
reasonable,
with
jackets
at 19,000esc,
skirts at
8,000esc
and suits
at 30,000esc.

Pied'poule

**Avenida de Roma, 38 B (D1)
☎ 21 847 94 27
Every day 10am-7.30pm,
Sat. 10am-1pm,
3.30-7pm
Amoreiras
and Colombo
shopping
centres (see
page 113).**

This is one
of three
shops in
Lisbon
belonging
to this
Portuguese
manufacturer.
Selling
clothes made
of fresh, cotton
fabrics in classic
shapes, as well
as co-ordinates
of every colour,
the choice is great
and the
prices are
affordable

(15,000–17,000esc for a dress,
20,000–25,000esc for a jacket,
and 8,000–10,000esc for a skirt
or trousers).

WOMEN'S ACCESSORIES – BAGS, GLOVES, HATS AND JEWELLERY

Portugal, the second largest manufacturer of shoes in the world, produces a range of shoes at a wide variety of prices. Good-quality handmade shoes are fairly expensive (but cheaper than at home) and there are plenty of more reasonable makes around. Accessories are important to the Portuguese, and bags, gloves, hats and jewellery are still made the traditional way. They may not always be the most fashionable, but they're very competitively priced.

BAGS

Malas do Rato

Largo do Rato, 9C
S. Bento/Estrela (B2)
☎ 21 387 38 33
Mon.-Fri. 9am-7pm,
Sat. 9am-1pm.

There are so many *malas* (bags) that you won't know which way

to turn, with handbags, shopping bags, rucksacks and briefcases of every colour and material (smooth and reversed leather, suede, fabric and vinyl). Most are made in Portugal and are affordably priced (5,000–8,000esc for a handbag with a leather outer, 10,000–15,000esc for a bag made entirely of leather, and excellent Italian bags starting at 20,000esc).

Pelusca

Praça da Figueira, 5
Baixa (C3)
☎ 21 347 60 96
Mon.-Fri. 9.30am-7pm,
Sat. 9.30am-1.30pm.

A narrow shop full of bags ranging from the traditional to the casual, with leather bags in navy and black, as well as shoulder bags in the latest summer colours for only 5,000esc. Although at that price only the outside is made of leather, they're still an ideal buy for the summer or for a special occasion.

Trudivora

Rua da Trindade, 28 (C3)
☎ 21 347 79 66
Mon.-Sat. 11am-2pm,
4.30-7.30pm.

This shop, with its grand Baroque interior, is housed in a magnificent *azulejo*-covered house in Largo Bordalo Pinheiro. Run by enthusiastic Spanish owners, it's filled with as many kinds of accessories as you could wish for. The selection of original, glamourous clothes is fantastic, and includes silk shoes, hand-painted scarves and 1920s-style jewellery.

GLOVES AND HATS

Luvaria Ulisses

Rua do Carmo, 87A
Chiado (C3)
☎ 21 342 02 95
Mon.-Fri. 9.30am-1.30pm,
2.30-7pm, Sat. 9.30am-1.30pm.

Luvaria Ulisses has the smallest shop window in Lisbon, and it's filled with *luvas* (gloves) for every occasion. There are *luvas* (gloves) for every occasion, in supple leather, reverse leather, suede and lace, in classic colours and fashionable shades, with or without stitching, from 5,000esc.

Place your hand delicately on the leather cushion on the counter and allow yourself to be gloved, but note that the shop's so small that only two people can enter at the same time.

Chapelaria Azevedo
Praça do Rossio 73 (C3)
☎ 21 342 75 11
Mon.-Fri. 9am-7pm,
Sat. 9am-1pm.

Chapelaria Azevedo is the traditional milliner of Lisbon. Why not pop along to take a look at this wooden shop and try on a few hats while you're there. They come in all shapes and sizes, from traditional *borsalinos* and panamas to special ceremonial hats that come with or without feathers.

JEWELLERY

Dom Pedro V Joias
Rua D. Pedro V, 9/11
Principe Real (C3)
☎ 21 343 38 45
Mon.-Fri. 10.30am-7.30pm,
Sat. 10.30am-2pm.

There are only a few objects on display here, but they're all very well chosen, including original designs by Vittorio Secco,

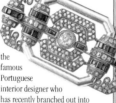

the famous Portuguese interior designer who has recently branched out into jewellery design. Inspired by the Portuguese discoveries, he blends the themes of land and sea with exotic inspiration from Macau and Japan, and combines gold in its various finishes and colours with precious and semi-precious stones.

Artefacto 3
Rua da Rosa, 158/160A
Bairro Alto (C3)
☎ 21 342 35 62
Mon.-Fri. 11am-1pm,
2-6pm.

The shop has been enlarged to incorporate the adjacent workshop, and you can now watch Alexandra, Paula, Teresa and a few other artists at work. They'll be delighted to show you the unique and unusual pieces they're making from precious and semi-precious metals. You're bound to find something here that you'll want to buy.

A LAND OF PURER GOLD

Portugal is one of the few countries in Europe where you can still find gold of more than 18 carats. A carat is a measure of the percentage of pure metal contained in an alloy and represents $1/24$ of the total mass. 24 carat gold is therefore pure, 18 carat gold is 75% pure and 19·2 carat gold is 80% pure. The 'Casa de Moeda Portuguesa' puts its *contraste* (stamp) on all the jewellery sold in Portugal, and this attests to the legality and purity of the metal (19·2 carats). Never buy jewellery without having checked that it bears the official *contraste*. Next to this stamp, you'll often find another one – that of the craftsman who made the piece, and sometimes even a third – that of the retailer.

If you're curious or just love jewellery, go to Rua do Ouro and the Chiado. For traditional jewellery try **Ourivesaria Sarmento**, Rua do Ouro, 251 (C3), ☎ 21 342 67 74, or **Ourivesaria Silva**, Praça Luis de Camões, 40 (C3) ☎ 21 342 67 74.

MEN'S FASHION AND INTERESTS

Lisbon may not be the capital of men's fashion, but there are still a good range of shops selling both modern and more traditional clothes, for work and for leisure, as well as accessories for every occasion. If you're feeling a bit more daring, there are excellent new Portuguese designers who are producing more fashionable and exotic clothes.

FROM HEAD TO TOE

Manuel Alves and José Manuel Gonçalves

Rua das Flores, 105 1°D (B3)
☎ 21 347 51 37
Mon.-Sat. 2-8pm.

José Antonio Tenente

Travessa do Carmo, 8 (C3)
☎ 21 342 25 60
Mon.-Fri. 10am-7pm.

If you like to wear fashionable and trendy clothes, then a new generation of Portuguese designers awaits you here.

Wander around José Antonio Tenente's shops and take in the audacious but well-cut jackets and shirts. Or make an appointment to visit the workshop of Manuel Alves and José Manuel Gonçalves who are known for their very daring styles.

Rosa and Teixeira

Av. da Liberdade, 204
Baixa (C2)
☎ 21 311 03 50,
📠 21 311 03 59
Every day 10am-7.30pm,
Sat. 10am-1pm, closed
Sun.

Cardoso Botelho

Av. da Liberdade 144-156
Baixa (C2)
☎ 21 347 22 55
Every day 10am-7pm,
Sat. 10am-9am,
3.30-7pm, closed Sun.

If you like smart, classic clothes, fine fabrics, (100% wool, cotton and cashmere),

perfect cuts, and are willing to spare no expense when it comes to quality, these are the shops for you. The wooden furniture, thick carpets and velvet-covered seats all add to the sumptuous atmosphere, and you can even have your suits and shirts made to measure.

SHIRTS OLD AND NEW

If you like to dress casually, but your favourite shirts are beginning to look their age, come along to the tiny **Hospital das Camisas** workshop, where you'll find piles of fabrics and shirts waiting to be repaired. If your collar or cuffs are a little frayed, or you want your long sleeved shirt altered to short sleeves, bring along your shirts and they'll come back transformed for an incredibly modest sum (900–1,200esc).

If you want to buy a new shirt that fits you really well, try **Mangas de Camisas**, where you'll find a choice of 350 different types of fabric waiting to be made into 25 different styles of shirt. Fast, economical service is guaranteed.

Hospital das Camisas,
Poço Borratem, 25 (C3)
☎ 21 886 34 02
Mon.-Fri. 9.30am-1pm, 3-7pm,
Sat. 9.30am-1pm.

Mangas de Camisas,
Largo Jean Monet, 1 Loja G
(off map)
☎ 21 355 67 43
Mon.-Fri. 10am-7pm.

Sapataria Presidente

Rua 1 de Dezembro, 9
Baixa (C3)
☎ 21 342 37 70
Mon.-Fri. 10am-7pm, Sat. 10am-1pm.

Sapataria Lord

Rua Augusta, 201 (C3)
☎ 21 346 10 13
Mon.-Fri. 10am-2pm, 3-7pm, Sat. 10am-2pm.

If you prefer wearing handmade shoes, then plan a visit to a Portuguese shoe shop while you're here. You won't necessarily find the styling of Italian shoes, but you can always count on the quality of the work. Try to find out where the shoes originate from – if it's S. João de Madeira (in the north of the country), then there's a good chance they were made entirely by hand from carefully-selected hides.

You can get a good pair of classic shoes for between 15,000 and 20,000esc.

SPORTY OR ACADEMIC?

100% Surf

Rua Coelho da Rocha, 20A,
Campo de Ourique (B2)
☎ 21 395 73 22
Mon.-Fri. 10am-7pm,
Sat. 10am-1pm, 2-7pm.

If you're keen on surfing you'll already have heard of the Guincho, the fine surfing beach a few

kilometres/miles from Lisbon (see page 69). If you've been longing to surf the Atlantic rollers but have left your board and wetsuit at home, don't worry. Just pop along to 100% Surf in Campo de Ourique, where you'll find everything you could possibly need, from Bermuda shorts and wetsuits to the latest boards. There also stock plenty of accessories, as well as some very colourful beach shirts.

find a large number of works by notable Portuguese authors such as José Saramango, the first Portuguese winner of the Nobel Prize 1998) or *The Book of Disquiet* (Fernando Pessoa), *The Maias* (Eça de Queiroz), *Happy Easter* (José Rodrigues Miguéis) and *Requiem: A Hallucination* (Antonio Tabucchi). The Livraria Bertrand has some books in English (generally translations of Portuguese authors) and some bilingual editions. The Livraria Britânica, catering for the nearby British Council, sells only English-language books.

Valentim de Carvalho

Praça D. Pedro IV, 55/59 (C3)
☎ 21 322 44 00
Mon.-Sat. 10am-8pm,
Sun. 11am-7pm.

Virgin Megastore

Praça dos Restauradores, 18/22 (C3)
☎ 21 346 03 09
Mon.-Sat. 10am-11pm,
Sun. 2-8pm.

Maritima

Doca de Santo Amaro (B3)
☎ 21 397 95 98
Every day 11am-8pm.

If you're a sailor at heart and long for the sea, you'll be in your element here. There's everything that you could wish for, including waterproofs, fishermen's sweaters and sea-faring caps, as well as tableware and accessories for your yacht. There's also a good selection of nautical artefacts and furniture with which you can decorate your home.

Livraria Bertrand

Rua Garett, 73 (C3)
☎ 21 346 86 46
Mon.-Fri. 9am-8pm,
Sat. 9am-10pm.

Livraria Britânica

Rua Luis Fernandes, 14 (C3)
☎ 21 795 68 66
Mon.-Fri. 9.30am-7pm,
Sat. 9.30am-1pm.

If you're a serious type who's never without a book and you can't get through the weekend without one, hurry along to one of these bookshops where you'll

Covering three floors, and offering an excellent selection of music, from Portuguese *fado* to the latest chart hits, the Virgin Megastore is

the place to come to if you are a music lover. If you want to try some real Portuguese music, here are a few suggestions: *Pedro Abrunhosa e Bandemonio* or *Xutos e Pontape* (rock), *V Imperio, Paulo Bragança* or *Madredeus* (modern *fado*), *Krywall* or *Cave Canem* (jazz/baroque), *Raul Marques e os Amigos da Salsa* (salsa) and *Fernando Marquês* (guitar).

Tertulia Festa Brava

Praça da Alegria, 38/C
Av. da Liberdade (C3)
☎ 21 342 42 52.

If you fancy trying your hand at bull-fighting, you can come along to Tertulia Festa Brava, one of the few bullfighting schools in the centre of Lisbon. Here the bulls are made out of wood and are mounted on castors. Tuition is free, and with a little luck you may be able to watch someone training and possibly even join in yourself.

Barbearia Fraga

Rua Milagres de
S. Antonio, 2 (D3).

This high-quality barber's is one of the best you'll find in the city. Located in the inspiring-sounding 'Street of the Miracles of St Anthony', a shave here is a most enjoyable and relaxing experience. A *corte and lavagem* (shampoo and cut) will cost around 1,500esc, a *corte de cabelo* (cut) costs around 1,100esc, and *barba* (a shave) costs 700esc.

BEER AND FOOTBALL — THE LADS' FAVOURITE WEEKEND

Choose your camp carefully, whether it be *azul, verde* or *vermelho*. Lisbon's rivals, Porto, play in *azul* (blue), Benfica play in *vermelho* (red) and Lisbon's other club, Sporting, play in *verde* (green). Football is the most popular sport in the city with regular league fixtures taking place on Sunday afternoons. After the match the local tradition is to head for the bars to enjoy the Portuguese beer. There are two of them on the market – Superbock and Sagres – they're both worth a try.

LISBON FOR THE LITTLE ONES

The Portuguese dote on their children, so don't worry if you're bringing your offspring with you, as they'll be treated like royalty. There are shops for *crianças* (children) everywhere, and plenty of activities to keep them busy.

CLOTHES AND SHOES

Bonchic

Rua Tomás Anunciação, 19-25 (B2)
Campo de Ourique
☎ 21 395 38 33
Mon.-Fri. 10am-7pm, Sat. 10am-1pm.

This is the outlet of a small, traditional workshop where everything is still handmade from lovely, soft fabrics such as cotton poplins and terry-towelling. The clothes for babies and toddlers (0–4 years) bear the workshop's Bolota label and include adorable smocked dresses for little girls and dungarees for little boys that you just can't buy at home (under 6,000esc). There are also some pretty accessories, including children's sheets, towels and wooden toys.

Cenoura

Amoreiras (see page 113), Colombo (see page 113) and Vasco da Gama (see page 65) shopping centres and Rua Augusta, 221 (C3)
☎ 21 342 46 77

Mon.-Fri. 10am-7pm, Sat. 10am-1pm.

If you don't want to dress your children in pale pink or blue, here's a great Portuguese make of children's wear that's not too expensive, and comes in bright, cheerful colours, often with flower or square motifs. It's grown-up fashion

in very small sizes (0–10 years), with matching accessories, such as socks and shoes. You'll also find maternity clothes in the same enchanting styles.

DECORATION AND TOYS

Dessempre

Rua Almeida and Sousa, 10A
Campo Ourique (B2)
☎ 21 386 40 22
Mon.-Fri. 10am-7pm, Sat. 10am-1pm.

The objects in this interior decoration shop are beautifully made in a traditional style, yet the colours are fresh and new. If you'd like to find a teddy bear like the one you had as a child or old-fashioned clothes like the ones you see in family photographs, Dessempre is the place to come. It's the ideal shop to buy presents for children (prices start at 2,500esc).

Os Ursitos

Av. da Liberdade, 245
Loja 7
Baixa (C2)
☎ 21 354 00 86.

The promise of the Spanish chain *Os Ursitos*, which has just opened a branch in Lisbon, is 'a dream bedroom for a dream child.' They've got everything here, from beds and chests of drawers to wallpaper and fabrics, plus a whole host of matching accessories, including lamps, coat pegs and picture frames.

You'll only find soft and pretty colours (powder blue and candy pink) in every shape and form, with spots, stripes, flowers and bows. All the furniture is made of white wood painted in the same pastel shades, with decoration in the form of teddy bears, rabbits, dolls, balloons and little cars. In other words, it's a dream world – except for the prices.

Abaco

Travessa Légua do Póvoa, Amoreiras (B2)
☎ **21 383 36 48**
Mon.-Fri. 10am-7pm,
Sat. 10am-1pm.

A large shop full of educational toys for children aged 2 to 8. There are lots of stimulating puzzles and wooden toys here, as well as all kinds of models to assemble. Abaco also has everything your child will need for painting and colouring, and there's even a large easel at the back of the shop for them to try things out on. If you have your

children with you, you may find it difficult to get them out of this shop.

P'ro menino and p'ra menina

S. Pedro de Sitra (off map)
☎ **21 923 18 37**
Tue.-Sun. 10am-7pm.

You have to search hard to find this charming shop, which is located at the back of a courtyard behind S. Pedro de Sitra marketplace, but there are so many tempting wooden toys that it's well worth the effort. Besides the building bricks, coloured letters and bedroom accessories, there are lots of little cars and other toys in great shapes and bright colours. It's like a child's dream come true.

Hopscotch – Oficina de Brinquedos

Av. dos Bombeiros, 16/A Estoril (off map)
☎ **21 466 53 79**
Mon.-Fri. 10am-7pm,
Sat. 10am-1pm.

Welcome to the wonderful world of Hopscotch, a mecca for doll's house collectors. Everything in the shop is in miniature. The houses are all beautifully decorated, with highly realistic-looking furniture and tiny accessories, including china tea sets, silver cutlery, hand-painted furniture and even household appliances that really work. The items are all one-twelth lifesize, including the dolls. A whole house will set you back at least 30,000esc, but you'll find many delightful and extremely tempting items for 1,000–5,000esc.

A WEEKEND IN LISBON WITH YOUNG CHILDREN

If you want everyone to enjoy themselves and avoid any whining, here are a few ways to combine your pleasure with theirs.

Museu do Brinquedo,
Rua Visconde de Monserrate
☎ 21 924 21 71, Tue.-Sun.
10am-6pm, entry charge.
You have to go down a rather steep staircase not far from the centre of Sintra to find this toy museum, which is tucked away in a fine 19th-century house. The two floors of toys of various periods and origins will delight all the family.

Museu das Marionetas,
Largo Rodrigues Freitas, 191
☎ 21 888 28 41, Tue.-Sun.
11am-7pm, entry charge.
You'll find marionnettes from all over the world in the heart of the most picturesque district of Lisbon. The short tour usually ends with a show.

Jardim Zoológico, Estrada de Benfica, 158 (B1), every day 9am-6pm (8pm in summer)
☎ 21 726 93 49, entry charge.
The zoo is situated in over 25 hectares/60 acres of magnificent gardens and allows you to combine a picnic and a visit to the zoo with a visit to the botanical gardens. There are dolphin shows every day.

Museu da Cera, Armazém 2, Doca de Alcântra (A3), every day 10am-8.30pm.
180 wax figures illustrating the important events in the history of Portugal.

AZULEJOS, PORCELAIN AND CERAMICS

The production of *azulejos* and tableware, one of the specialities of Portuguese craft, is a thriving business. Alongside reproductions of antique items, you'll find an incredible variety of objects that are resolutely contemporary in design, in terms of both their patterns and colours.

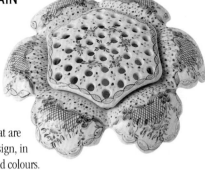

Azulejos Sant'Anna

**Rua do Alecrim, 95
Chiado (C3)
☎ 21 342 25 37
Mon.-Fri. 9.30am-7pm,
Sat. 10am-2pm.**

This is the outlet of the Sant'Anna factory, one of the few factories that originated in the 18th-century still in operation today. Everything here is handmade in the traditional way. You'll find panels, copies of antique designs and decorative objects. Framed puzzles consisting of 4–9 tiles sell for 12,000–20,000esc.

The workshop in Belém is also open to visitors.
Sant'Anna,
Calçada da Boa Hora, 96-E
☎ 21 363 82 92,
Mon.-Fri. 9am-12.30pm,
1.30-6pm, closed Sat.

Azulejos Santa Rufina

**Calçada Conde Panafiel 9/A
Castelo (off map)
☎ 21 887 60 17
Tue.-Fri. 10am-1pm, 3-5pm.**

A real old-fashioned workshop that's fairly difficult to get to as you have to climb the Calçada do Conde Panafiel. However, once you arrive at the top, you can see how inspired the artists must be by the amazing view from the workshop windows. Santa Rufina mainly produces reproductions of antique tiles, but also offers training.

Fabrica Viuva Lamego

**Largo do Intendente Pina Manique 25
Mouraria (off map)
☎ 21 885 24 08
Mon.-Fri. 9am-1pm, 3-7pm,
Sat. 9am-1pm, closed Sat.
Jul.-Aug.
Calçada do Sacramento, 29
Chiado (C3)
☎ 21 346 96 92**

**Mon.-Fri. 9am-7pm,
Sat. 9am-1pm.**

It's worth going along to see the Viuva Lamego factory in the Mouraria (founded in 1849) for its marvellous *azulejo* façade alone. It boasts one of the finest examples of 19th-century *azulejos*, which was executed by the master of the art, Ferreira das Tabuletas, with allegorical representations of trade and industry. With a little luck, you'll also be able to see the artists at work. The pieces on display are all reproductions of 17th- or 18th-century works (around 13,000–15,000esc for a framed panel of 4 tiles). You can also find tableware here, and if you have a specific design that you want to have made up, they will make it to order.

Ratton

**Rua Academia das
Ciências, 2C
Bairro Alto (B3)
☎ 21 346 09 48
Mon.-Fri. 11am-1pm, 3-6pm.**

Not just a shop, Ratton is also an art gallery, proving that *azulejos* are a living art form and that the traditional craft still inspires contemporary artists. You may be lucky enough to chance on an exhibition here by Paula Rego or some other famous Portuguese painters.

Ceramica Cintra Antiga

**Rua da Ferraria, 13,
Vila Velha, Sintra (off map)
☎ 21 923 57 01.**

Azul Cobalto

**Calçada de S. Pedro,
S. Pedro de Sitra (off map)
☎ 21 923 54 84.**

In Sintra, you'll probably see artists at work in one of the many small workshops that are still operating in the town. You can watch the painters making careful copies of 17th- or 18th-century pieces, or executing whole canvasses before your very eyes. Each of the two workshops has its own style and it is worth taking a look in both of them.

SPAL Porcelanas

**Centro Comercial das
Amoreiras, Loja 2083
Amoreiras (B2)
☎ 21 383 20 36
Every day 10am-11pm.**

Along with Vista Alegre, this is the other great manufacturer of Portuguese porcelain. SPAL, or the Sociedade de Porcelanas de Alcobaça, may be a little less prestigious than its close competitor, but it's certainly still worth your attention. As a specialist in tableware, producing some 55,000 pieces a day in a state-of-the-art factory, SPAL recently received permission from the National Museum to reproduce items from its collections, which has led to a whole series of objects that make delightful little presents,

CERAMICS, POTTERY AND EARTHENWARE

Nearly every region in Portugal produces some kind of ceramics, pottery or earthenware (see page 18). Among the more famous are the pots of Alentéjo, whose warm terracotta colour is combined with blues and dark greens, the finer earthenware of Coimbra, with its elaborate motifs, and the tableware of Alcobaça and the Sintra region. It's up to you to decide which you prefer to take home. You can find them at

Mercearia Liberdade,
Av. da Liberdade 207
☎ 21 354 70 46 (C3).

Santos Oficios,
Rua da Madalena, 87
☎ 21 887 20 31 (C3).

A Zé,
Rua das Padarias, 13
Vila Velha, Sintra (off map)
☎ 21 923 11 62.

Solar, Rua Consiglieri
Pedroso, 6, Sintra (off map)
☎ 21 924 82 45.

including an ashtray depicting the Lisbon trams (2,800esc) and a coffee set illustrating the great discoveries (a gift set consisting of six cups and six saucers costs 9,500esc).

LINEN AND LACE

Portugal is without a doubt the home of household linen. Using techniques that have been passed down over the centuries, cotton and linen are finely embroidered in a number of regions in Portugal. Bobbin lace is made in many of the northern towns, and soft, thick terry-towelling is made a hundred or so kilometres (60 miles) from Lisbon.

HOUSEHOLD LINEN

Auri

Av. de Roma, 36B (D1)
☎ 21 849 54 60
Mon.-Fri. 9.30am-7pm,
Sat. 9.30am-1pm.

This traditional shop, which still retains an old 19th-century cash register, has an excellent selection of household linen. There are *turcos* (towels) of every size and colour from Torres Novas, a town north of Lisbon that specialises in terry-towelling (large towels cost around 3,000esc, small towels cost around 1,200esc and guest towels cost around 450esc). These are reasonable prices to pay for a high-quality makeover for your bathroom. You'll also find some pretty embroidered tablecloths by Viana do Castelo.

Parisemlisboa

Rua Garett, 77 (C3)
☎ 21 346 88 85
🄵 21 346 81 44.

A fascinating shop with three floors of beautiful household linen. If you're looking for a romantic, old-fashioned trousseau, go straight to the second floor where you'll find hand-embroidered nightdresses, sheets and tablecloths, as well as household goods made from 100% linen. You'll find marvellous (100% cotton) fabrics on the top floor and masses of towelling products on the first, most of it made in Torres Novas, the Portuguese home of towels. They're wonderfully soft and thick and the range of colours is sufficiently wide for you to be sure to find one to go with your

bathroom. Treat yourself to a complete set of bath towels, (around 2,800esc each), hand towels (around 950esc each) and guest towels (around 650esc each).

Teresa Alcerim

Rua Nova de Almada, 76 (C3)
☎ 21 342 18 39
Mon.-Fri. 10am-7pm,
Sat. 10am-1pm
Centro Comercial das
Amoreiras, Av. Duarte
Pacheco (see page 13).

This is the shop to come to for small, tasteful presents as there's plenty to choose from at reasonable prices. A linen tea cloth or guest towel costs 600–1,200esc, monogrammed towels cost around 1,500esc, and there are plenty of table mats and tablecloths. Not only will you be spoilt for choice, but everything comes beautifully gift-wrapped in colourful paper with a pretty ribbon.

O Bragal

**Centro Comercial Libersil,
Loja 46
Av. da Liberdade, 38
Baixa (C2)
☎ 21 342 51 78.**

This attractive shop, hidden away in the heart of the Libersil shopping centre, is worth searching out. You'll find all the Companhia de Torres Novas's towelling articles here, including bathrobes for 6,000–7,000esc and sets of towels for 5,000–6 000esc. Take a look at the children's sheets and baby linen embroidered in cross-stitch. Their old-fashioned charm is so hard to resist that it's not surprising they've come back into fashion.

Pano Branco

**Rua do Patrocinio, 49
Campo de Ourique (B3)
☎ 21 395 02 55
Mon.-Fri. 10am-1pm, 3-7pm,
Sat. 10am-1pm.**

This tiny shop is very welcoming, with its old-fashioned wooden shelves overflowing with linen. The colours are soft and the fabrics are 100% *algodon* (cotton) or *linho* (linen). There are large plain or patterned tablecloths

(2m50x 1m50/100inx60in) priced at 12,000–15,000esc and matching napkins at around 5,000esc for 6, bath towels for 3,000esc, large towels for 1,500esc and small towels for 550esc. There's also everything you could need for your baby, including bedding, towels and delightful bathrobes with hoods, provided you're looking for the traditional pale pink or blue.

Casa Branca

**Praça da Republica
(off map)
☎ 21 924 48 94
Every day 10am-7pm.**

This is the latest shop selling fine linen to open in Sintra. There's plenty to tempt you here, including beautiful embroidered sheets, towels, bedspreads, teacloths and hand-embroidered cotton and linen table napkins. You'll find everything is produced in light colours, such as white, ecru, beige and cream. It's the kind of linen you can't buy at home now, and although it's expensive, it's well worth coming for.

Turcos
and Bordados

**Rua Ferreira
Borges, 149 A
(B2)
Campo de
Ourique
☎ 21
385 24 50
Mon.-Sat.
10am-7pm.**

Ideally you should bring your entire trousseau along to this shop-cum-workshop to have it personalised. It's one of the few places that combines the quality of traditional

methods with modern techniques. Thanks to a computerised system, you can have any type of letter or design embroidered (350esc for capital letters and 100esc for small ones). If you haven't got your household linen with you, console yourself by choosing something from the collections on display. There are two qualities of towelling (400 and 500g/m^2/14 and 18oz/sqyd) and four sizes of towels in over twenty colours. You're sure to find something you like.

INTERIOR DECORATION

The Portuguese pay special attention to the interior decoration of their homes, preferring warm materials such as wood, elaborate shapes including wrought-iron designs, and colourful, draped curtains. They have a good eye for detail, and traditional craft objects are often found alongside contemporary design. With an excellent range of interior decoration shops, Lisbon is a wonderful place to stock up on ideas and objects for your home.

Loja da Atalaia
Rua da Atalaia, 71
Bairro Alto (C3)
☎ 21 346 20 93
Every day 2-8pm, closed Sun.

Only high-quality and very expensive items are on show in this furniture display gallery. Sofas, tables and chairs from the 1950s sit side-by-side with older, valuable Portuguese and foreign pieces. Genuine Murano glass vases by Venini have pride of place on the tables, but it's probably better not to ask the price! You'll be made to feel welcome here whether you're a buying customer or just browsing for ideas.

Tom Tom Shop
Rua do Seculo, 4
and 13/15/17
Bairro Alto (C3)
☎ 21 347 97 33
Mon.-Fri. 1-8pm,
Sat. 11am-7pm

This is the ideal place to buy all the accessories you need for your high-tech kitchen. Why not check out the colourful tablecloths for decorating your picnic table in the summer? There are also some very original photograph frames, ranging from flamboyant Baroque designs to the kitsch and if you can't bear to be parted from the picture of your loved one, even when you're in the bath, choose an inflatable frame that floats. A second shop has recently opened opposite which sells very stylish, contemporary furniture and objects.

FINE TABLEWARE

The Portuguese are now producing much sought-after tableware, thanks to a combination of quality, modern styling and price.

Cutipol

Rua Alecrim, 115 (C3)
☎ 21 322 50 75
Mon.-Fri. 10am-7pm,
Sat. 10am-1pm.

This major Portuguese brand of cutlery has given itself a makeover, reflected in its shop's designer decor, light wooden furniture, frosted glass shelves and soft lighting. The range of cutlery has been extended with some very modern designs. T he Madison range, for example, has been very successful with trendy restaurants all over the world , Expect to pay around 2,150esc for a knife, 1,120esc for a fork or dessert spoon and 1,100esc for a teaspoon.

Atlantis

Rua Ivens, 48 (C3)
☎ 21 321 93 38
Mon.-Fri. 10am-7pm,
Sat. 10am-1pm.
Sparkling Portuguese crystal, including glasses (2,500–4,500esc), carafes (12,000–15000esc) and other affordable small articles.

Vista Alegre,

Largo do Chiado, 28, and
Casa Alegre,
Rua Ivens, 58 (C3).
The most famous Portuguese porcelain factory (see page 41).

Vermelho de Março

Rua do Seculo, 104
Bairro Alto (C3)
☎ 21 343 12 23
Mon.-Fri. 1-8pm,
Sat. 11am-7pm.

The decor of this shop is quite something in itself, with its bare wooden floor, pastel colours,

patinated wood, and antiqued and coloured wrought iron. You'll find a few original ideas, such as pretty bud vases to hang on the wall, (from 2,800esc) and painted wooden frames. The furniture has a fresh look too, with a brick-red or off-white limed finish.

Lartenautica

Centro Cultural de Belém (off map).
Tue.-Sun. 11am-2.30pm, 3.30-8pm.

If you're a sailor at heart, you can stock up on a plethora of nautical items in this fascinating shop, and redecorate your home to simulate an ocean-going ship. There are porthole mirrors, nautical fabrics, knots you can't unravel, ships in bottles, furniture and navigational instruments including compasses. Although you won't find many antiques here, they're definitely all the genuine article.

Semnome

Rua Antonio Mario Cardoso, 64, Chiado (C3)
☎ 21 342 99 81
Mon. 3-8pm, Tue.-Fri. 11am-2pm, 3-8pm,
Sat. 11am-2pm, 3-6pm.

This shops sells amazing handles made of different materials in all shapes and colours, which will add new life to your chest of drawers or kitchen cabinets. You can buy a handle in the shape of suns, moons, jellyfish or starfish made of resin or metal (around 2,200esc each) to personalise your wardrobe or drawers. Semnome also stocks other novelty items and is certainly worth a detour when you're out shopping in the Chiado.

Mar & Mar

**Rua Antonio Mario
Cardoso, 70
Chiado (C3)**
☎ 21 343 04 78
Mon.-Fri. 11am-8pm,
Sat. 11am-1pm, 3-6pm.

It's impossible to cross the
threshold of this appealing shop
without coming back out laden
with parcels. Shades of blue
blend with soft greens and bright
orange to form a harmonious
setting for a variety of furniture
and household objects. There are
colourful ceramic plates (made
in Alentéjo using traditional
techniques, but contemporary
designs and colours), original
table mats, frames, candlesticks,
photograph albums
and heaps
of affordable
objects
starting at
3,000esc.

Vivamus

**Praça de Londres, 8
Avenidas (D1)**
☎ 21 847 48 34
Mon.-Fri. 10am-7pm,
Sat. 10am-2pm.

The saffron-yellow sponged walls
set the tone of this interior
decoration shop, where
the accent is on goods
from the south of
Portugal and on
the sea. Here
you'll find
netting dotted
with shells
which will
create a real
maritime feel in
your home, as well
as lots of natural
wood and painted
frames for your favourite
pictures (around 3,000–
5,000esc each).

Etamine

**Avenida de Roma, 42 A/C
Avenidas (D1)**
☎ 21 847 25 20
Mon.-Fri. 10am-1.30pm,
2.30-7pm, Sat. 10am-1.30pm.

You'll find everything you could
possibly want for your home on
the two floors of this shop. There
are marvellous little Baroque and
Classical style frames, wooden
trays and

colourful tablecloths, as well
as fabric sold by the metre and
small items of painted wooden
furniture. You may also be
tempted to splash out on one
of the huge dishes or another
piece of tableware from Alcobaça
(a city to the north of Lisbon that
produces fine ceramics) or even
a whole dinner service (1,800–
2,100esc for a plate and
6,000–8,000esc for a dish or
a salad bowl).

Manueis

**Rua Federico Arouca, 91
Cascais (off map)**
☎ 21 483 34 52
Mon.-Fri. 10am-7pm,
Sat. 10am-1pm.

At Manueis, a shop in Cascais,
you'll find a good selection of
items for the home. The carefully-
arranged room sets include a
bedroom with a wrought-iron
bed, an Arraiolos carpet and
marvellous fabrics, as well as a
beautifully designed bathroom.
The shop includes some
original ideas, paper,
cardboard and
wooden storage

FURNISHING FABRICS

The Portuguese love fine fabrics and dress their windows with curtains in original styles and colours. You may find they resemble English fabrics to a certain extent. Wander round and be inspired by ideas for drapes to give your windows a festive air. Most of the fabrics come in 1m50/60in widths at relatively attractive prices (2,000–4,000esc a metre). If you're thinking of making curtains, you'll need to measure the width of your windows and the drop required before leaving home. For tablecloths, allow 20–30cm/ 8–12in extra on each side of your table, and for 6 napkins, allow around a metre of fabric. Here are two essential shops in the Campo de Ourique district.

Santo Contestavel,
Rua Saraiva de Carvalho,
354C (B2)
☎ 21 396 38 41,
Mon.-Fri. 10am-7pm,
Sat. 10am-1pm.

José Manuel Vidal,
Rua Saraiva de Carvalho,
356B (B2)
☎ 21 397 54 86,
Mon.-Fri. 10am-7pm,
Sat. 10am-1pm.

boxes, traditionally-styled towels, coloured linen teacloths and objects for the kitchen and bathroom.

Antonio Eduardo Dias

Rua Consiglieri Pedroso, 11
Sintra (off map)
☎ **21 923 51 94**
Every day 10am-6pm,
closed Sun.

This isn't a shop but a workshop, where wrought-iron objects are made to measure. Bring along your designs for a garden set, a small Baroque table for your sitting room, or a grand headboard for your bed. The objects are attractively priced, but check in advance how much your design will cost to make, so you are sure that it's really worth it once you've also paid for the cost of transportation.

ANTIQUES, ART AND *VELHARIAS*

Lisbon has a reputation for being an ideal spot for bargain-hunters, and the number of antique shops, second-hand shops and booksellers is quite impressive. Rare pieces unfortunately sell for unusually high prices, while cheap *velharias* (bric-a-brac) are seldom worth buying.

ANTIQUES

Intermobilia (R. Quintela and F. Moncada and J. Andrade)

Rua Escola Politecnica, 39 Principe Real (C2/3)
☎ 21 342 49 64
Mon.-Fri. 10am-7pm,
Sat. 11am-1pm.

This large antique gallery is a feast for the eyes, with its superb collection of 19th-century Portuguese furniture, paintings, old porcelain and authentic wooden sculptures. It's a good place to get a *Santo da roca* dating from the 19th century – a type of wooden model with a porcelain head representing a saint, which were dressed and paraded during the popular processions. They're original pieces that can't be found elsewhere, and the smallest of them are still affordable.

Galeria da Arcada

Rua D. Pedro V, 56 (C3)
☎ 21 346 85 18
Mon.-Sat. 10am-1pm,
3-7pm.

Over the years, Portuguese religious artists have produced a large number of painted wooden sculptures representing popular saints or the Virgin and Child. In this antique shop specialising in religious objects, you'll find magnificent 17th-century multi-coloured sculptures, as well as small statues of St Anthony, St Vincent and St Joao – but all at high prices.

Nobre

Rua de S. Bento, 224 and 386/388 S. Bento (B2)
☎ 21 396 12 27
Mon.-Fri. 10am-1pm, 3-7pm,
Sat. 10am-1pm.

Whatever you want, whether it's an old record-player, an Art Nouveau vase, a small Gallé lamp or a 1930s or 1940s sideboard or chairs, rummage around in one of these two shops and there's a good chance you'll come up with what you're looking for at a reasonable price.

BOOKS AND ENGRAVINGS

O Mundo do Livro

Largo da Trindade, 11 (C3)
☎ 21 346 99 51
𝟋 21 347 08 04
Mon.-Fri. 10am-7pm,
Sat. 10am-1.30pm

This is the best-known shop in Lisbon for engravings. Rodrigues Pires is a specialist, and people come to consult him from all over the world – he's even been decorated

by the president of Italy himself. Incredibly knowledgeable about all aspects of engravings, he answers experts and tourists alike with the same smile. There are three floors of original engravings dating from the 16th, 17th and 18th centuries, on every imaginable subject and at a very wide range of prices (8,000–150,000esc), as well as a remarkable collection of maps that includes some very rare specimens. You'll also find an impressive

AUCTIONS (*LEILÕES*)

For true connoisseurs, who are looking for a rare piece and are ready to pay the price, there are several auction rooms in Lisbon. A catalogue (for which there is a charge) is available a few weeks before the auction and can be ordered by telephone or fax. The lots are put on show 4 to 5 days before the sale and some auction rooms have late nights, when they stay open until midnight. On the day of the *leilão* (sale), it's important to arrive on time in order to get a seat.

Cabral Moncada Leilões,
Rua Miguel Lupi, 12 D
(S. Bento)
☎ 21 395 47 81
🖷 21 395 51 15.
Mon.-Sat. 10am-midnight,
Sun. 3-8pm.

Soares & Mendonça,
Rua Luz Soriano, 53-1°
(Bairro Alto)
☎ 21 342 13 12
Mon.-Fri. 9am-1pm, 3-7pm.

amount of excellent-quality hand-coloured reproductions, with prices starting at 2,000esc.

Livraria Barateira
Rua Nova de Trindade, 16 C
Chiado (C3)
☎ 21 342 67 55.

Livraria Olisipo
Largo Trindade Coelho, 7/8
Chiado (C3)
☎ 21 346 27 71
Mon.-Fri. 10am-7pm,
Sat. 10am-1pm.

These are two great places to find engravings and old books of every kind. You may be lucky enough to come across a beautifully-bound rare edition of your favourite author, or copies of old magazines with yellowed photographs that will satisfy your taste for nostalgia. Rummage around and you may come up with an inexpensive find.

ART GALLERIES

Stuart
Rua Nova do Almada, 20-22
Chiado (C3)
☎ 21 342 21 31
Mon.-Fri. 10am-7pm,
Sat. 11am-1pm.

At last, an art gallery where you can buy good, local paintings at affordable prices. The contemporary paintings by rising young Portuguese and foreign artists aren't exactly cheap, but you'll also find an interesting series of watercolours of Lisbon at prices to suit most pockets. An excellent way to remember the delights of this beautiful city.

VELHARIAS

Feira da Ladra
Campo de Santa Clara
S. Vicente/Graça (D3)
Tue. and Sat.

Brocante du Parque das Nações
Pavilhão do Portugal
(off map)
2nd and 3rd Sun. in the month, 10am-7pm.

These two flea markets couldn't be more different. The Feira da Ladra, the oldest flea market in Lisbon, is held around the metal covered markets of the picturesque Campo de Santa Clara district. Although the name means the 'Thief's Market', it's in no way a den of thieves but a real bric-a-brac market. It offers more in the way of atmosphere than bargains, and has nothing in common with the second-hand market of the Parque das Nações, which is favoured by collectors.

Mercado de S. Pedro de Sintra
Sintra (off map).

A large market is held in Praça de S. Pedro de Sintra on the second and fourth Sunday of the month. Clothes, fruit and vegetables, as well as a wide variety of *velharias,* are on sale here. Rummage away to your heart's content and you may come up with a 16th-century *azulejo,* an interesting piece of tableware or some lovely old engravings in reasonable condition. You may not always find a great bargain, but you're bound to have an enjoyable day out.

GASTRONOMIC SPECIALITIES

The Portuguese love their food and are particularly proud of their pastries. Make sure you try the local produce while you are in Lisbon – the charcuterie of Alentéjo, the cheeses of the Serra and the regional wines, which are often surprisingly good.

A Casinha do Pão

Centro Comercial das Amoreiras
Av. Duarte Pacheco
Loja 3001
Amoreiras (B2)
☎ 21 385 85 36
Every day 10am-11pm.

You could easily pass by this small shop window and tiny counter without really noticing them,

but pay attention, as it would be a pity to miss all the delicious cakes that they sell here. It's a good place to stop for something sweet to eat as you wander round the Centro Comercial das Amoreiras, but you may find it very difficult to choose from the tempting selection. Besides the *bolos de cannèle* (cakes with walnuts),

orange and lemon-flavoured *pasteis de nata* (custard-cream

pastries), *queijadas* (cheesecake) and *queques* (cakes), there's delicious *pão de lo* (a very light Genoa cake). If you really can't make up your mind, have a *sortido do dia* (assortment of the day).

Napoleão

Rua dos Franqueiros, 70
Baixa (C3)
☎ 21 887 20 42
Mon.-Sat. 9am-8pm.

Napoleão has a wide range of wines and port and the staff are used to serving tourists, so you'll easily find someone to explain to you in English everything you ever wanted to know about Portuguese wine. The wines are classified by region and it's easy to tell them apart. If you're offered some wine to taste, you can accept without hesitation as there's no

obligation to buy. If you decide to make some serious additions to your cellar, you can have wine delivered to your home.

O Rei do Bacalhau

Praça da Figueira, 2B
Baixa (C3)
Mon.-Fri. 9am-7pm,
Sat. 9am-1pm.

The 'king of cod', as he is known by his regulars, sells all kinds of cod in his authentic shop which is located right in the city centre. If you want to make *bacalhau com natas* (salted cod with cream) when you get home, ask for some good, thick *postas* (pieces) and wrap them up well in plastic for the journey back.

Martins and Costa

Rua Alexandre Herculano, 34
Av. da Liberdade (C2)
☎ 21 314 16 17
Mon.-Fri. 9am-7pm,
Sat. 9am-1pm.

You can only just see this delicatessen, hidden under the tall trees of Rua Herculano near the Avenida da Liberdade. It stocks an excellent assortment of Portuguese wines, including quality ports and madeiras, which may have something to do with the fact that it's located on the opposite side of the street to the wine institute. It's also a great place to buy the traditional accompaniments that go with your wine, such as *queijo da Serra* (ewe's cheese) and a delicious *presunto pata negra* (raw country ham).

Celeiro

Rua 1 de Dezembro, 65
Baixa (C3)
☎ 21 342 24 63
Every day 9am-7pm.

This delightful health food supermarket only sells organic produce. You can find all you need for a macrobiotic diet here – a riot of fibres and cereals, soya, medicinal plants and essential oils. Everything's guaranteed 100% natural. You can also try out their vegetarian specialities in the restaurant on the floor below,

where you'll find a canteen atmosphere, with a mixed clientele sipping the organic fruit and vegetable juices and enjoying a wide choice of dishes that are healthy without being dull. Delicious vegetable tarts, quiches and spring rolls, all for under 1,000esc each.

O Espirito do Vinho

Rua Ferreira Borges 94B
(B2)
☎ 21 385 90 78
📠 21 395 67 65
Mon.-Sat. 10.30am-8pm.

This is another wine merchant's that has opened recently in Lisbon. For some time now, the Portuguese wines have been advertising their quality and variety, aided in their efforts by the dynamic marketing

A NICE CUP OF *TSCHA*

The first Portuguese to arrive in Canton were delighted to discover a mystical ritual and a purifying drink, *tscha*. The Chinese word *ch'a* describes a medicinal plant that's been used for over 4,000 years.to purify the body and sharpen the senses. It is, of course, none other than tea, and in around 1520 it made its way back to Portuugal along with many other spices. It's said to have crossed the Channel to England in 1662, when Catherine of Bragança married Charles II, and brought her tea with her. If you want to buy *tscha* or *chà* in Lisbon (as well as some good blends of coffee), the place to go is:

Casa Pereira
Rua Garett, 33 (C3)
☎ 21 342 66 94
Mon.-Fri. 9am-7pm,
Sat. 9am-1pm.

methods of the wine institute and by the growing number of connoisseurs who dream of restoring the reputation of Portuguese wine. It's also the aim of this shop, which offers a wide choice of the best national wines, as well as wine-related items, expert advice and courses in oenology (the study of wine) and wine-tasting.

MARKETS AND SHOPPING CENTRES

Traditional markets and ultramodern shopping centres exist side-by-side in Lisbon. Fortunately, the Portuguese craze for shopping malls, which are springing up in the outskirts of the city, don't seem to have had the slightest effect on attendance at the old-fashioned covered markets, which continue to offer a delightful selection of fresh, local produce.

MARKETS

Mercado de Carcavelos

Carcavelos, every Thu., 9am-1pm
Trains every 15 mins from Cais do Sodre to Oeiras and Cascais (off map).

A jumble of market traders and stalls, the crowd is so dense in places that you can hardly make any headway. Hawkers spread their wares on the ground between the pathways and official stands, only to run off at the first sign of a policeman's peaked cap, while the barrow boys shout out their wares from the safety of the stalls. You can come here to experience the atmosphere,

but there are also real bargains to be had. You can find well-known brands that are slightly imperfect or have miraculously escaped the normal distribution channels (between 1,500–3,000esc a garment), as well as Alcobaça tableware at around 1,000esc for three plates, and cotton bedspreads straight out of the pages of *Homes and Gardens* magazine for a ridiculously low price.

Mercado da Ribeira
Cais do Sodré (C3).

The big covered markets of the city were moved to a large domed metal structure in Cais do Sodré in the 1930s to free up the Praça da Figueira. There aren't many big markets left in the capital cities of Europe today, so make sure you visit the ones in this area before they're turned into a giant shopping centre. The warehouses down by the river are a hive of activity from 1am onwards as lorries bringing fruit and vegetables arrive from all over the country. On the city side, there's the market, which you should visit early in the morning if you want the freshest produce.

Mercado Municipal de Campo de Ourique

**Rua Padre Francisco,
Rua Coelho da Rocha (B2)
Mon.-Sat. 7am-1pm.**

This is one of the best stocked of all the municipal covered markets. It's still the popular meeting-place for locals and the various corporations are grouped together in the big covered market, with the fishmongers in Rua Padre Francisco, the butchers in Rua Coelho da Rocha and the fruit and vegetable sellers in between. You will quickly see that only vegetables in season are on sale here, and that they come from proper vegetable gardens where the use of fertilisers is still relatively unknown (although they may not be labelled organic).

Mercado das Flores

**Cais do Sodré (C3)
Mon., Wed. and Fri.
7.30-8.15pm.**

At 7.30pm there are queues in front of the gates of this flower market, and forty minutes later there's nothing left. If you love flowers, you mustn't miss the slot between the wholesale market (in the afternoon) and closing time. Public opening time is limited to a short 45 minutes, but it's enough for you to have your head turned by the scents and colours of the fresh bouquets. Everything is sold off for a few hundred escudos, and you could

fill a whole house with flowers without ruining yourself. It's ideal if your plane's leaving in the next few hours.

Mercado do Peixe

**Travessa de S. Miguel
Tue.-Sat. 9am-1pm.**

Every morning, the fishermen come to sell their fish and *mariscos* (seafood) in the heart of the Alfama. With its well-organised street displays, it's the meeting-place of the housewives of the district, and is both picturesque and authentic.

SHOPPING CENTRES

Vasco de Gama

**Avenida D. João II,
Parque das Nações (off map)
☎ 21 895 52 85
Every day 10am-midnight**

Colombo

**Av. Lusíada, Benfica (off map)
☎ 21 711 36 00
Every day 10am-midnight**

Oeiras Parque

**Av. A. B. Cabral de Macedo,
Oeiras (C2)
☎ 21 446 00 50
Every day 10am-midnight**

Atrium Saldanha

**Praça Duque de Saldanha (C1)
☎ 21 319 22 50
Every day 10am-10pm.**

Das Amoreiras

**Av. Eng. Duarte Pacheco (B2)
☎ 21 381 02 00
Every day 10am-midnight**

The Centro Comercial das Amoreiras, nicknamed the 'Amo', used to have people from all over the country flocking to it, but it now faces stiff competition. The opening in September 1998 of Colombo, the biggest shopping centre in the Iberian Peninsula (140,000m²/1,500,000sqft with 500 shops) marked the start of a new era for shopping centres in Portugal. A number have since opened their doors, including the Atrium Saldanha in the centre of the modern city, Oeiras Parque between Lisbon and Cascais, and Vasco da Gama on the site of Expo '98 which, like Colombo, is the property of the largest distribution group in the country (Sonae). These centres have become the favourite shopping haunts of the inhabitants of Lisbon.

BARGAIN CORNER

The fashion for *segunda mão* (second-hand goods) is beginning to catch on in Lisbon. The Portuguese used to only aspire to things that were new and perfect, labelled with a well-known (preferably foreign) brand name. But despite experiencing unprecedented economic growth since joining the European Union, the country continues to suffer social problems and high unemployment, and people are realising that by buying second-hand goods they can continue to shop without financial ruin.

Stockissimo

Travessa do Enviado da Inglaterra, 7A, Av. da Liberdade (C2)
☎ 21 314 27 22
Mon.-Fri. 10am-7pm, Sat. 10am-3pm.

Stockissimo became a victim of its own success, and was forced to leave its pretty but small shop in the Chiado for one three times larger. The collections have now been extended and include fashionable clothes by Max Mara, Kenzo, Betty Barclay etc. In terms of lingerie, there's Warner, Huit, Benetton and Calvin Klein, not to mention swimsuits, accessories and silk scarves by Yves Saint-Laurent and Ferragamo. All clothes are reduced by between 40 and 80%.

Mme Bettencourt

Rua Nova da Trindade, 26 1°D (C3)
☎ 21 342 53 16
Mon.-Fri. 9am-1pm, 3-7pm.

Dona Fernanda's shop is an institution in Lisbon and she's been offering a choice of nearly-new clothes for over fifty years. It may take you a while to locate the shop and to find something you like, but it's worth the effort, if only because it's such a very picturesque place.

Gardenia

Rua Morais Soares, 93A, Loja 10, Galerias 80 (D2)
☎ 21 347 06 11
Mon.-Sat. 10am-7.30pm.

This is the outlet for seconds from the Gardenia design workshop. Here you can find not only the rising young generation of Portuguese designers, from Nuno Gama to Fatima Lopes, but also many other more or

less well-known fashion designers. A good selection of trendy clothes in a boldly designed shop.

El Dorado

Centro Comercial das Amoreiras, Loja 1030 (B2)
Av. Duarte Pacheco
Amoreiras
☎ 21 383 18 36
Mon.-Sun. 11am-11pm.

El Dorado is home to a collection of second-hand clothes from the 1970s. Here you'll find close-fitting garments made from synthetic fabrics, bell-bottom trousers, paisley shirts, tank tops and psychedelic jewellery. If you want to stock up for your next fancy-dress party, just browse around and you might find that turquoise sequined dress or fuchsia pink feather boa that you've always wanted – all for less than 10,000esc!

Mandrake

Calçada do Combro, 11/13 (C3)
☎ 21 342 50 76
Mon.-Sat. 10am-8pm.

If you're nostalgic for the 1970s, make a note of this shop as it's one you really shouldn't miss. Jean-Pierre offers you nearly-new clothes in very good condition, including skirts, blouses, jeans and a whole range of accessories. With all the colourful ideas, you can easily give yourself a makeover without breaking your budget.

Rés-Vés

Rua Ferreira Borges, 98B (B2)
☎ 21 385 26 36
Mon.-Fri. 10am-1.30pm, 3-6.45pm,
Sat. 10am-1pm.

You'll find anything and everything here, and if you love rummaging, then you will be in your element. It doesn't matter

what you're looking for, as you're sure to come up with something you like, whether it's old records, lace straight from someone's attic, second-hand clothes, shoes, tableware or any other item from the strange assortment of disparate objects found here.

Bozart

Rua Francisco Metrass, 53A (B2)
☎ 21 397 72 06
Mon.-Sat.
10am-1pm, 3-7pm.

Bozart offers a wide range of shoes and bags at unbeatable prices. The shop naturally refuses to say where the goods come from, but they're almost certainly unsold items from previous years or bankrupt stock.

Don't tell everyone, but believe it or not, you can get a pair of women's shoes here from only 899esc.

Nightlife Practicalities

If you feel like an evening out, dress up to the nines and take in an opera at the *Teatro São Carlos* or a concert at the *Coliseu*. Or if you'd rather mingle with the crowds, go and see a *Tourada,* or wander from bar to bar in the narrow streets of the Bairro Alto. If you're feeling nostalgic, drown your sorrows in *saudade* in the Alfama. And if you like trendy clubs, discover the world of the '*muito in*' – night-owls – in the Docas d'Alcântara, Avenida 24 de Julho or Jardim do Tabacco. But if you're simply feeling romantic, enjoy a candlelit dinner on the Tagus.

the tourist information office. These are two valuable guides to what's happening in Lisbon during the current month, covering shows, museums, concerts, bars, restaurants, discos and hotels, as well as a selection of shops. They're free and *LISBOAem* is bilingual, in English and Portuguese. You'll also find the review *Follow Me Lisboa* (in English) at the airport and in some hotels. It summarises Lisbon's main attractions each month (from restaurants and monuments to shops and shows).

FINDING OUT WHAT'S ON

Since its launch in September 1998, the review *City*, with its magazine format, well-informed articles, pertinent critiques and unbeatable guide to what's on in the city, has become the bible of Lisbon life. If you want to know everything that's happening in the city during your stay, *City* is the magazine for you. The dailies *O Publico*

and *O Diario de Noticias* give practical information about theatre and cinema programmes each day, as well as a list of useful phone numbers. *Espresso* (a weekly that is published on Saturdays) offers two tabloids, *Cartaz* and *Vidas*, which provide a complete overview of shows and exhibitions, along with comments. You can also get the *Agenda Cultural* and *LISBOAem* free from

WHERE TO GO

For about the last three years, Lisbon has been experiencing its own Portuguese-style *Movida*. Like Madrid in the 1970s, a wild, young crowd are discovering the the excitement of living in a city that throbs with life into the early hours. You only have to go to one of the two or three districts that are home to Lisbon nightlife at the weekend to be sure of it. In the patchwork of steep narrow streets of the Bairro Alto, you'll find one fashionable restaurant, typical bistro, tourist-filled *fado* club and trendy disco after another. From 11.30pm, the streets are filled with little groups of people drinking beer while a few yards away, the Casa de Fado touts for tourists for the next show. Much later on in the evening, night-owls cluster round the doors of the clubs and discos. The Cais do Sodré, Avenida 24 de Julho, Les Docas and brand-new Jardim do Tabacco district, where the trendiest bars, pubs and discos can be found, are the places to be on a Friday or Saturday night. The atmosphere is completely different from that of the Bairro Alto. Disco-bars with the most fantastic decor, ranging from minimalist design to the wildest Baroque, have been opened in former warehouses. Clubbers vie with one another in the eccentricity of their fashion to gain entry to these temples of techno. There's no point in arriving before midnight. The Baixa is home to most of the theatres, but don't expect to find much happening, or even any restaurants open in the district after the show.

BOOKING SEATS FOR A SHOW

You can book seats for most of the shows in the neighbourhood of Praça dos Restauradores.
ABEP (next to the metro exit) every day. 9am-6pm. Be prepared to pay cash. You can also book by phone: ☎ 21 342 53 60,

Virgin Megastore (at no. 7, ☎ 21 346 03 09), takes credit cards.
You can also try:
Fnac Colombo (☎ 21 711 42 00, every day 10am-midnight). You'll pay a commission wherever you go, but it's the easiest way to book – most of the theatres don't take phone reservations. As a last resort, go direct to the box office of the theatre in question before the show.

FINDING A BABY-SITTER

In case you've decided to take advantage of the Lisbon nights to go out on a spree, here are the numbers of two baby-sitting agencies.

Pedroso & Lino
☎ 21 793 47 93
Intess
☎ 21 888 25 06.

SUMMER FESTIVALS

From late May onwards, don't miss the music festivals, which often include open-air concerts. The **Lisbon Festival** (late May to late June) includes theatrical performances, open-air concerts and fireworks.
The **Sintra Music Festival** (mid-June to mid-July) features concerts of classical music in the region's palaces (Palacio Nacional de Sintra, Palacio da Pena, Palacio de Queluz, etc.). For information call ☎ 21 923 48 45.
The **Sintra Classical Dance Festival** (the whole of August) features performances by companies

from all over the world at the Palácio de Seteais in Sintra. Even if you're not normally interested in dance, the sumptuous setting of the Palácio de Seteais (now a luxury hotel) is well worth an evening of your time. For information and reservations call ☎ 21 923 32 00.
The **Fundação Calouste Gulbenkian open-air concerts** (generally the first week in August) feature jazz concerts in the Parque de Palhavá auditorium, Avenida de Berna, 45 A .

LIVE MUSIC

Some bars and restaurants stage live concerts (*ao vivo*) all year round. This is true of the cafeteria of the Centro Cultural de Belém, O'Gilin's Irish Pub, the B. Leza, as well as restaurants such as the Speakeasy, the Blues Café, the Salsa Latina and many others.

THEATRES, CONCERTS, OPERA, DANCE

There are numerous theatres and show venues in Lisbon and you should usually be able to get seats at the last minute. For classical concerts and ballet, consult the programme of the Fundação Calouste Gulbenkian. For contemporary music and dance, try the Centro Cultural de Belém, Coliseu or Culturgest, and for theatre, look at the programme of S. Carlo or D. Maria.

Fundação Calouste Gulbenkian
Av. da Berna, 45
☎ 21 793 51 31
Box office: ☎ 21 797 41 67

Internet www.gulbenkian.pt
Reservations at box office, 1-7pm
Seats for concerts 2,000–3,000esc, for dance 2,000–5,000esc.

The Fundação Calouste Gulbenkian has one of the richest programmes of classical music in Lisbon. It has its own philharmonic orchestra and ballet company, as well as being host to various foreign companies on a regular basis.

Centro Cultural de Belém
Praça do Imperio, Tram 15
☎ 21 361 24 00
Box office: ☎ 21 361 24 44
Reservations: every day 1-9.30pm (by telephone except on day of performance)
Seats for concerts 1,000–3,000esc, for dance 2,000–5,000esc.

The Centro Cultural de Belém probably has the most eclectic programme of performances of any of the venues. It includes plays, classical music, jazz and contemporary music, operatic recitals, modern dance and musical comedies. There are performances by the Portuguese symphony orchestra, with concerts from April to June.

Parque Mayer

Situated in a little street that crosses Avenida da Liberdade, Parque Mayer is not a park, but a theatre. In the late 19th century, the industrialist Alfredo Mayer had the old theatres on the site renovated. It's here that the Portuguese *revistas* (revues) developed following a similar style to the shows that were flourishing in Paris at the time. They praised the beauty of Lisbon and were critical of the political life of the period. Parque Mayer still exists and ,along with popular theatres, such as the ABC and the Teatro Maria Vitoria, still stages *revistas*.

Parque Mayer, Travessa do Salitre (Metro Avenida). Shows Sat. 8.30pm and 11pm, Sun. 4pm and 9.30pm, seats 1,200–3,500esc.

Teatro ABC
☎ 21 343 01 03.

Teatro Maria Vitoria
☎ 21 346 17 40
(reservations unnecessary).

Coliseu dos Recreios
Rua das Portas de Santo

Antão, 92-104
☎ 21 346 19 97
Reservations every day
1-8.30pm
Seats 2,000–8,000esc.

The Coliseu dos Recreios is *the* indoor venue specialising in concerts of rock and pop music. A beautiful old domed building, it's the place to see foreign artists and groups, such as dEUS, Gaetano Veloso and Bryan Adams perform when they're on tour. The Coliseu also sometimes plays host to foreign opera companies.

Teatro São Carlos

Rua Serpa Pinto, 9
☎ 21 346 84 08
Seats 3,500–40,000esc
(box for four).

The Teatro São Carlos is the home of Lisbon opera.

Unfortunately the season is very short (only from February to June), and there are few performances which means tickets are in great demand. On top of this, you can't get seats at the ABEP kiosk and it's almost impossible to get the theatre on the phone, so the only thing you can do is try your luck at the box office.

Pavilhão Atlântico

Parque das Naçõ,
Alameda dos Oceanos
Reservations: ABEP kiosk,
FNAC, Virgin Megastore
or at box office on day of performance
Seats 5,000–20,000esc.

This is Lisbon's new large concert hall and was the Utopia Pavilion during Expo '98. Now that it's been opened, the city is at last in a position to stage rock and pop concerts on an international scale. Booking is essential, as seats are in great demand despite the high prices.

Culturgest

Rua do Arco Cego
☎ 21 790 10 65
Reservations (48 hrs before start of performance):
☎ 21 790 51 55
Box office: Mon.-Fri. 1-7pm
Seats 1,200–3,000esc.

Designed by the architect Arsenio Cordeiro in 1993, this building is amazing both in its size and conception. It's the head office of the Caixa Geral de Deposito (the Portuguese funding body for public works and housing). It's also a cultural centre specialising in the contemporary arts that stages exhibitions, high-quality jazz concerts and film shows.

The Lisbon Players

Rua da Estrêla , 10
☎ 21 396 19 46

If you're feeling really homesick, you may want to try out the Lisbon players, a group of mainly

Praça de Touros

Campo Pequeno
☎ 793 21 43
Jun.–mid-Oct.
Seats 1,500–9,000esc
Tourada at 10pm.

The Portuguese *touradas* (bullfights) are much less bloody than their Spanish counterparts. as the bulls aren't actually killed in the arena but are slaughtered in the bull pen after the fight. The circling of the *cavaleiros* (horse-men) in their splendid costumes is a spectacular part of the event.

ex-pat actors, who give regular readings and performances.

Cinema

The city has dozens of cinemas, usually showing original-language films with Portuguese subtitles. To find out what's on, consult the listings at the APEB kiosk or enquire at the Tourist Office (see also page 117).

BARS, CAFÉS AND LIVE MUSIC

To take full advantage of the city's nightlife, you should head for the Bairro Alto or the dockland districts: Cais do Sodré, Docas de Alcântara, Avenida 24 de Julho and the Doca do Jardim do Tabacco in particular. You'll find that many bars offer good, quick and cheap meals, as well

as staging live music concerts at the weekends. If you want to liven up your evening, try a shot of the local spirits or brandy.

Bairro Alto

Café Targus
Rua Diario de Noticias, 40B
☎ 21 347 64 03
Every day 10-2am,
closed Sun.

Café Targus is one of the best bars in the district and offers a designer decor and exhibitions of contemporary works by young

Portuguese artists. If you fall in love with any of the paintings you can buy them from the owner, Hermani – they're all for sale. Try one of the barman's many cocktails, but don't bother going until at least 11pm as the bar only gets busy later on.

Work in Progress
Rua da Bica Duarte Belo,
47/49 (Elevador da Bica)
☎ 21 346 14 86
Every day noon-2am.

A short distance from the traditional night-time circuit of the Bairro Alto, Work in Progress (known as WIP) is a place

unlike any other – it's a hairdresser's as well as a bar. From noon you can have a cup of coffee at the counter (ask for '*uma bica, faz favor*'), and then entrust your hair to the professionals. If you're bored with your present look, and fancy a change, then this is the place for you. You could even enjoy a Marguerita while you wait for things to hot up at the end of the evening.

Café Geronte
Travessa da Boa Hora, 5
☎ 21 346 80 95
Sun.-Fri. 1pm-2am.

This is an odd kind of a secondhand bookseller's, as it's not only a shop but also a bar that serves *petiscos* and drinks, accompanied by good background music. Take a careful look on the shelves and you'll find plenty of bargains for around 200esc. On Mondays and Thursdays, bands provide live music for the evening.

Avenida 24 de Julho

Trifasica
Av. 24 de Julho, 66
☎ 21 395 75 76.

The Trifasica, the T-Clube of Lisbon and José Manuel Trigo's Algarve all have the same metallic design, the same inevitable billiards table and the same smart, trendy clientele. It's the place to go for a drink while you're waiting for the neighbouring discos to open. With prices ranging from 2.50 to 12esc, why not try a few of the beers from their extensive selection.

Cais do Sodré

A Capela
Rua da Atalia, 45
☎ 21 347 00 72
Every day 9pm-3am.

Housed in a former chapel, as indicated by the vault and statue of St Anthony, A Capela is one of the trendiest bars of the moment. It no doubt owes its success to the team which runs it. Pedro Silva, its young owner, knows what his customers want, and provides a lively, trendy venue. The two Fernandos, who share the role of DJ, are experts in the art of sound, providing music to which you won't be able to stop dancing.

O'Gilin's Irish Pub
Rua dos Remolares, 8
☎ 21 342 18 99
Every day 11-2am.

One of Lisbon's thriving Irish pubs, the atmosphere here is very convivial and its the perfect place for Irish brunch on a Sunday morning, or a bite to eat if you've slept until the early afternoon (meals are served from 11am to

5pm). On Friday and Saturday evenings, there's live music from a rock or jazz group to end the evening, and the rest of the week the owner provides the entertainment by chatting to the customers. If you're in Lisbon on 17 March, don't forget it's St Patrick's Day, and you can join in unmissable celebrations in all the Irish pubs.

Alcântara/Docas

Salsa Latina
Gare Marítima de Alcântara
☎ 21 395 05 50
Every day 12.30pm-3am.

If you've always wanted to learn to dance the salsa, there's only one place try – Salsa Latina. The food is really good here (see page 76) and there are salsa lessons every Friday evening. There's also live music every evening at 10pm, with a second group after midnight at the weekend. It has a marvellous setting just outside the docks, and from the dancefloor you can admire the beautiful view over the Tagus as you party till the early hours of the morning.

Speakeasy
Rocha Conde de Obidos,
Cais das Oficinas,

Armazem 115
☎ 21 396 42 57
Every day noon-4am.

Every evening after 11pm, this bar-restaurant undergoes a transformation as the crowds arrive. It's known for its excellent jazz concerts, and the

trumpet player Laurent Filipe, one of the four owners of the place, takes care of the programming so nothing is left to chance You're sure to find a high-quality group every evening, with excellent jam sessions every Wednesday evening.

Rock City

**Rua Cintura do Porto
de Lisboa,
Armazém 225
☎ 21 342 86 40.**

If you like T-bone steaks, an American atmosphere, electric guitars and rock, you'll love this place. Even if you arrive before the start of the concert, the background music will get you in the mood. If it's fine, choose a table in the tropical garden beside the Tagus for dinner, but if you don't want to miss a minute of the show, take up a position close to the stage or on the mezzanine.

Avenida da Liberdade/ Principe Real

Hot-Clube de Portugal

**Praça da Alegria, 39
☎ 21 346 73 69
Tue.-Sat., 8pm-2am.**

This legendary cellar is one of the most famous jazz clubs in Lisbon and deserves its excellent reputation. It's ideal for jazz fans who are looking for great music and it certainly lives up to its name, as you may find yourself escaping to the cool of the courtyard. Come any day from Tuesday to Saturday as there's sure to be a good act on stage, and enjoy a Sagres (beer) or a glass of wine as you listen to the hot sounds.

O Chafariz do Vinho

**Rua Mae de Agua,
Praça da Alegria
☎ 21 342 20 79.**

Lisbon's first wine bar is located in the renovated setting of a former *chafariz*, one of the old fountain reservoirs that supplied the city with water at the start of the 20th century. According to João Paulo Martins, a specialist wine journalist and a partner in the business, it's the ideal place to store wine, as the 400m/yds of tunnel always stay at the perfect temperature. The beauty of the setting also makes it the ideal place to enjoy a glass or two of wine. After close on a century, the taps of the *chafariz* are flowing again, but this time with wine rather than water.

S. Bento

Foxtrot

**Travessa de Santa Teresa, 28
☎ 21 395 26 97
Sun.-Thu. 6pm-2am,
Fri.-Sat. 6pm-3am.**

The decor of this bar is reminiscent of the 1930s. Don't be put off if the two small sofas in the first room are already taken, just take a wander into the other rooms or the little inner garden. Between the enormous velvet

sofas and the bistro seats, you're sure to find somewhere cosy to sit where you can enjoy a *caipirinha*.

Alfama

O Salvador

**Rua Salvador, 53
☎ 21 887 19 70
Every day 9pm-2am.**

Don't be alarmed if the blue and white walls of this attractive little bar begin to sway after a few drinks, as the cocktails can be quite explosive! Elixirs such as the 'Blood of Christ' and the 'Virgin Mary' may taste heavenly and sound innocent enough when you order them, but don't be surprised if you wake up with a headache the next day.

CLUBBING

As with the late bars, the best parts of Lisbon to go to for clubbing are the Bairro Alto and the Zona Ribeirinha, or riverside districts (Docas – docks, Avenida 24 de Julho and Cais do Sodré). The clubs and discos officially open at around 11pm and there's either an entry charge (1,000–10,000esc) or you have to buy a drink (900–5,000esc). Don't expect to find much in the way of atmosphere before midnight, and even less to dance to before 1am. Remember that for the city's true night-owls, it's a must to party until *pôr-do-sol* (dawn).

Avenida 24 de Julho

Kapital

Avenida 24 de Julho, 68
☎ **21 395 59 63**
Every day 10.30pm-4am.

This is one of the most popular clubs in Lisbon, if the queues to get in at the weekend past the discriminating bouncers are anything to go by. The entry charge (10,000esc) is a form of selection in itself. On some evenings you may see a famous Portuguese footballer or other celebrities among the trendy, yuppy clientele. The three floors offer different kinds of music and atmosphere in a stark, black and white decor. On the first floor, you'll find techno (except on Wednesdays, which are

devoted to hard rock), on the second there's a bar where you can chat, and on the top floor there's another dance floor with a fine view of the river.

Kremlin

Escadinhas Praia, 5
☎ **21 395 71 01**
Wed.-Sat. 2-7am.

Probably the club with the most interesting history in Lisbon. the building is said to be connected to a secret network of tunnels running under the city. It was originally built as a convent in the 18th century, but was later converted into a prison, before becoming an aerobics centre and finally the new 'in' place for trendy young people. The crowds nowadays don't come for the inspired setting and, with its wild decor and youthful clientele, the Kremlin is one the city's most popular nightspots and the home of techno in Lisbon. Be warned, however, it's not easy to get past the bouncers.

Plateau

Escadinhas Praia
☎ **21 396**
51 16
Tue.-Sat.
10.30pm-6am.

If you like the Baroque style, you'll love the Plateau, which is another of the city's legendary nightspots. With gilded columns and Classical and neo-Classical frescoes, it's a feast for the eyes. It also remains true to its original vocation – rock – which attracts an audience of faithful fans. Some *caras* (faces) will seem familiar to anyone who's acquainted with Portuguese television.

Alcântara and Docas

Dock's Clube

Rua da Cintura do Porto de Lisboa, 226
Rocha Conde de Obidos
☎ **21 395 08 56.**

If techno is not your scene, and you'd prefer to dance to some

good old 1950s rock 'n roll, sway to the sound of the reggae beat, listen to some 1960s tunes or hark back in time to the sounds of the 1970s, then Dock's Clube is the place for you. The enormous, plush velvet sofas and comfortable armchairs will allow you to sip your cocktail at leisure before stepping out onto the dance floor. You won't be able to chat much to your friends though, as the music here is always extremely loud.

Benzina

Travessa Teixeira Junior, 6
☎ 21 363 39 59
Every day
midnight-
4am.

This fashionable club is said to be the favourite haunt of artists. People like to watch the dancers on the dance floors from the mezzanine and try to pick out the person they're supposed to be meeting. With a smart chrome and wood decor, there's nothing unusual in regards to the music here, with techno every day except Wednesday, when there are special 1960s and 1970s evenings.

Cais do Sodré

Bar do Rio

Cais do Sodré, Armazem, 7
☎ 21 346 72 79
Every day 11pm- 6am.

A waterside bar with a comic book decor. This former riverside warehouse has been given a makeover and now sports deep red walls, aggressive yellow lighting and green beams, with lifesize posters of comic book characters as decoration. Here you can sip your cocktail in a deckchair under an enormous fan, then take to the dance floor and dance the night away to what passes for the most 'in' music in the capital. Another late-night spot that only really gets going after midnight.

Belém

T-Clube Discoteca

Edifício Espelho d'Agua
Avenida da Brasilia
☎ 21 301 66 52
Every day. 10pm-4am.

T-Clube is a classy restaurant with a very well-established reputation (see page 80) that becomes a disco in the small hours. There's a ruthless selection at the entrance and it's better not to turn up without a tie, though your Gold Card may get you in. You'll pass a pleasant but predictable evening here.

Bairro Alto

Fragil

Rua da Atalaia, 126/128
☎ 21 346 95 78
Mon.-Sat. 10.30pm-4am.

En route to Cape Verde and Africa

If you like the music of Cape Verde and Africa, Lisbon has a number of treats in store for you.

B-Leza, Largo do Conde Barão, 50, 2° ☎ 21 396 37 35, Tue.-Sat., 11pm-7am. On the 1st floor of a 16th-century palace that must have seen more aristocratic occasions in its former life, you'll find a room with marvellous ceilings. If it doesn't seem a very promising place at first, it means you've arrived too early as it doesn't really have any atmosphere until around 2am, when the regulars arrive at this popular club.

Ritz Club, Rua da Gloria, 57 (Av. da Liberdade) ☎ 21 342 51 40, Tue.-Sat. 10.30pm-3.30am. Another of the city's legendary music venues, Ritz Club is Lisbon's largest African club and is housed in a slightly old-fashioned former tavern.

Another name that connoisseurs may find interesting is that of the very trendy **Kudissanga**, where they have a very strict door policy and excellent African music (Rua Carlos Reis, 51, Avenidas ☎ 21 393 33 55, 1pm-4am.

Gay nights

According to the national weekly *Expresso*, nearly 90% of Portuguese gay men live a double life, essentially family men in the daytime, but 'coming out' at night. In Lisbon, there are about twenty bars and discos with a mainly gay clientele – most of whom are men with high incomes, and their *escudos cor de rosa* ('pink escudos'), are gladly welcomed by the clubs they frequent. Whether you're gay, lesbian or straight, you'll be welcome in most of the following places, provided you know how to enjoy yourself.

Trumps

Rua da Imprensa Nacional, 104B ☎ 21 397 10 59, Tue.-Sun. 11pm-4am. One of the classic gay venues for over 15 years, it's known for its disco and drag shows.

O Finalmente

Rua da Palmeira, 38 ☎ 21 347 26 52, every day 10.30pm-4.30am. A well-known club with weekend drag shows at 2am.

Memorial

Rua Gustavo Sequeira, 42 A ☎ 21 396 88 91. The only club in the city that caters solely for lesbians.

Kings and Queen's

Rua da Cintura do Porto de Lisboa, Rocha Conde de Obidos, ☎ 21 397 76 99. This is one of the latest clubs to open in Lisbon and is very popular.

The Fragil has changed a great deal since its owner Manuel Reis, better known as the *senhor da noite*, defected to the banks of the Tagus and built his new mecca, the Lux,

there. Fragil, housed in a lovely old building, used to be one of Lisbon's trendiest and most pretentious clubs, and the new management are trying to reclaim some of its former glory. For them, as for all fans of the Bairro Alto, this is quite a difficult move at a time when the docks are the fashionable place to be seen.

Doca do Tabacco

Lux

Doca Jardim do Tabacco
Rua G. Matos Sequeira, 42
☎ 21 882 08 90
Mon.-Sun. 11pm-4am,
Thu.-Sat. 11pm-8am.

What happens when the king of the Lisbon nightlife, Manuel Reis, decides to sell his legendary club, the Fragil, and open up a new temple to music on the Jardim do Tabacco dock opposite Santa Apolonia station? Barely six months after it opened, it's already becoming a legend. There's no doubt about it, this new disco has a brilliant future ahead of it.

FADO HOUSES

For the first-time visitor to Lisbon, *fado* is a must. The only problem is that the shows are mostly intended for tourists. Some places still claim to be staging *fado vadio* (amateur *fado*), however no-one is guaranteeing its authenticity, not even the local enthusiasts who proclaim loudly that *'fado vadio morreu hà muito tempo!'* (*fado vadio* died out long ago'). You can still hear *fado* in a smart, well-known club or in a cosy, family bistro.

Bairro Alto

A Severa

Rua das Gaveias, 51
☎ 21 346 40 06
Mon.-Sun. 8pm-2am,
closed Thu.

The walls of this district's somewhat classy *fado* house tell the tragic tale of Maria Severa, a young nineteenth-century gipsy girl who sang the most extraordinarily beautiful *fado*. She was as famous for her

captivating voice as for the ravages she inflicted on the hearts of society men. Her stormy affair with the Conde de Vimioso, and her premature death at the age of 26 were a source of inspiration for all the court poets. Her house is the obvious place to stage performances of the rather melodramatic *fado*.

house liquers with evocative names, such as *shot de maça* (literally 'apple shot') and *moranguinho* ('little strawberry').

Alfama

Parreirinha de Alfama

Beco Espirito Santo, 1
☎ **21 886 82 09**
Mon.-Sat. 8pm-2am.

One of the most famous clubs in Lisbon is run by the *fadista* Argentina Santos and is lined with photos of the greatest *fado* stars. This guarantees not only the quality of the voices but also entitles you to the company of groups of tourists.

Down *fado vadio* way

Here are a few popular places where the local amateurs come to sing live around midnight. You won't always get a seat, but it's the price you pay for the old-fashioned charm and they're still very authentic, despite what people may say.

Adega do Ribatejo
Rua Diario de Noticias, 23,
☎ 21 346 83 43.

A Mascotte da Atalaia
Rua da Atalaia, 13, ☎ 21 347 04 08, Mon.-Sat. 8pm-3am.

Clube de Fado
Rua S. João da Praça,
☎ 21 888 26 94.

Arcadas do Faia

Rua da Barroca 54-56
☎ **21 342 67 42,**
Ⓕ 21 342 19 23,
Mon.-Sat., 8pm-2am.

Even if you're not the only tourists to frequent the place, you'll still get good value for money, with traditional, plentiful cuisine and high-quality singers and musicians. If you want an enjoyable, if slightly melancholic evening, this is the place to come.

Os Meninos

Rua Diario de Noticias, 68
☎ **21 346 93 23**
Every day 10pm-3.30am.

Unlike most of the traditional *fado* clubs, Os Meninos isn't also a restaurant. The decor is unpretentious and simple and the club has an authentic *fado* atmosphere with a touch of the foxtrot thrown in. It isn't frequented much by tourists but is more like a local café, where people come to chat. It's an interesting experience that you can complete by trying the

Come on weekdays or after dinner, when it's a little more authentic.

Lapa

O Senhor Vinho

Rua do Meio, 18 (Lapa)
☎ **21 397 26 81**
Mon.-Sat. 8.30pm-3.30am
(*fado* from 10pm).

This is another well-known venue, thanks to the fame of its owner, Maria da Fé, the great Portuguese *fado* singer. You have to wait until the end of the various sessions to hear her perform, which won't be before midnight. It doesn't matter, though, as the other singers (such as Jorge Fernando, Carlos

Macedo and Maria Dilar) will have captivated your heart in the meantime. The tourist set meal at 7,000esc per person is expensive but plentiful, with a few good specialities, such as *bacalhau a Senhor Vinho* and *cataplana de lotte* thrown in.

This guide was written by **Catherine Tanneau Cremonesi**, who would like to thank Claire Baudoin, Maria Helena Carnet, João Catel-Branco Pereira, Tomas, Collares Pereira, Isabel Corte Real, Pedro Luis da Costa Gomes Lopes, Rosaria Dantes, Martin Edwards, Isabel Freire, Luisa Romão, João P. Salazar Leite and José Sancho Silva.
Translated and edited by **Margaret Rocques**.
Series editor **Liz Coghill**.
Additional research and assistance by **Marie-Caroline Dufayet**, **Hélène Firquet, Jeannine Goulhot, Claire Wedderburn-Maxwell, Jenny Piening** and **Christine Bell**.

We have done our best to ensure the accuracy of the information contained in this guide. However, addresses, phone numbers, opening times etc. inevitably change from time to time, so if you find a discrepancy please let us know. You can contact us at: hachetteuk@orionbooks.co.uk or write to us at Hachette UK, address below.

Hachette UK guides provide independent advice. The authors and compilers do not accept any remuneration for the inclusion of any addresses in these guides.

Please note that we cannot accept any responsibility for any loss, injury or inconvenience sustained by anyone as a result of any information or advice contained in this guide.

Photo acknowledgements

Inside pages
© **Éric Guillot**: pp. 3 (t., c. l., b. r.), 11 (t. l., c. r.), 12 (b. l., c.), 13 (t. l.), 14 (t. r., c. l., b. r.), 15, 16 (t. r., b. c.), 17, 18, 19, 20, 21, 22, 23, 25 (t. c., b. r.), 26 (t., c., b. r.), 27, 28, 29 (t. l., t. c., b. r.), 30, 31, 32, 33, 34, 35, 36, 37 (t. c., c. r., c. l.), 38, 39, 40, 41, 42, 43 (t. l., c., c. r.), 44, 45, 46 (c. r., b. r.), 47, 48, 49, 50 (b. l.), 51 (t. r., c. c.), 52 (c. l., c.), 53 (c., c. r., b. r.), 54, 55, 56, 57, 58, 59 (c. l.), 60, 61, 62 (c. r.), 65 (b. c.), 66, 67 (t. c., c. r., b. r.), 68, 69 (c., c. l., b.), 72 (c., c. r.), 73, 74 (t. l.), 78, 79, 80 (b. r.), 82, 83, 88, 89, 90, 91 (c., c. r.), 92, 93, 94 (t., c. r., b. l.), 95 (t., c. r.), 96, 97, 98, 99, 100, 101, 102 (t. r., c., b. l.), 103 (t. l.), 104, 105 (c.l., b. r.), 106 (t. r., b., t. l.), 108, 109, 110, 111, 112 (c., b. l.), 113 (c.), 114 (c. l., b. r.), 115 (c. l., b. r.), 118 (t. l., b. r.), 119, 120, 121, 122, 123, 125, 126 (t.)
© **Christian Sarramon**: pp. 2, 3 (c. r.), 12 (t. r., c. r., b. r.), 14 (c.), 25 (b. l.), 46 (c. l.), 50 (c. r.), 51 (b. l.), 59 (c. t.), 74 (c., b. r.), 77 (t.), 80 (c. l.), 113 (c. r.), 118 (c. r.)
© **Jacques Debru**: p. 16 (c. l., c. r.), 17 (t. l.), p. 69 (t. r.), 112 (b. c.), 113 (t. l.)
© **Laurent Parrault**: pp. 53 (t. r.), 81 (b.), 94 (b. r.), 95 (b. l.), 114 (t.), 115 (t., c. r., b. l.)
© **Patrick Sordoillet**: p. 102 (c. l.), 103 (b. r.)
© **Nicolas Edwige**: p. 65 (c. c.)
© **Hachette**: pp. 10, 11 (c., b. r.), 24, 29 (c. b.)
© **1997-Parque Expo 98 S. A.**: p. 65 (t. r.)
© **Ask Images**: S. Labrunie: p. 64, S. Attal: p. 120 (t.)
© **Hémisphères – Stéphane Frances**: p. 62, Bruno Barbier: p. 63 (t. l., b.), Pawel Wysocki: p. 67 (t. l.)
Acquarela: p. 26 (b. l.), **A Ginjinha**: p. 37 (b. r.), **Pavilhão Cinês**: 52 (b. l.), **Hôtel Britania**: p. 72 (b. l.), **As Janelas Verdes**: 75, **Restaurante Comida de Santo:** p. 77 (b.), **Lidija Kolovrat**: p. 91 (b. l.), **Violeta:** p. 101 (c.), **Pano Branco:** p. 101 (b. l.), **Laternautica**: p. 105 (t. r.), **Manueis**: p. 107 (t.), **Pinto Leite:** p.107 (b. l.), **Senhor Vinho:** p.126 (c., b. l.)

Front cover.
Éric Guillot: t. l., c. c., c. r., b. l.
Stock Image: b. c. foreground, Anna Rossi t. c. foreground, C. Bouvier c. r. foreground,
Christian Sarramon: t. r., c. l., b. r.

Back cover.
Éric Guillot: t. r., b. l., c. foreground, **Christian Sarramon:** c. l.

Illustrations: Monique Prudent

First published in the United Kingdom in 2001 by Hachette UK

© English Translation, Hachette UK 2001
© Hachette Livre (Hachette Tourisme) 2000

Distributed in the United States of America by Sterling Publishing Co., Inc.
387 Park Avenue South, New York, NY 10016-8810I

A CIP catalogue for this book is available from the British Library

ISBN 1 84202 011 0

Hachette UK, Cassell & Co., The Orion Publishing Group, Wellington House, 125 Strand, London, WC2R OBB

Printed and bound in Italy by Milanostampa S.P.A.

If you're staying on and would like to try some new places, the following pages give you a wide choice of hotels, restaurants and bars, listed by district with addresses.

Although you can just turn up at a restaurant and have a meal (except in the most prestigious establishments), don't forget to book your hotel several days in advance (see page 70). Prices given are a guide only. Enjoy your stay!

STAYING ON
A LITTLE LONGER

The following hotels are listed strictly in accordance with the official Portuguese classification. Prices are given for a double room with en-suite bathroom or shower and breakfast. These are high-season prices, and should be used as a guideline only. If you go during the low season, you can pay significantly less. For additional information on hotels in Lisbon, see Rooms and Restaurants (page 70).

Baixa/Avenida da Liberdade/Saldanha

Avenida Palace★★★★★
Rua 1º de Dezembro, 123
☎ 21 346 01 51
🄵 21 342 28 84
38–55,000esc.
This former 18th-century palace in the historic centre of Lisbon has just been completely redecorated and has become one of the most charming of the big luxury hotels.

Ritz★★★★★
Rua Rodrigo da Fonseca, 88
☎ 21 383 20 20
🄵 21 383 17 83
43–59,000esc.
This is without a doubt the hotel with the most prestigious list of clients, including French President Chirac on his last visit to Lisbon. Luxury rooms with a good view of the Parque Eduardo VII.

Sheraton Towers★★★★★
Rua Latino Coelho, 1
☎ 21 357 57 57
🄵 21 354 71 64
39–53,000esc.
This hotel offers not only the predictable comfort of a chain with an international reputation, but also one of the finest views of the city from the terrace on the top floor.

Sofitel★★★★★
Avenida da Liberdade, 123
☎ 21 342 92 02
🄵 21 342 92 22
35–40,000esc.
This hotel is very well-situated on the most famous avenue in Lisbon. It offers pleasant, spacious rooms, and the very copious breakfast buffet is worth staying for.

Tivoli★★★★★
Avenida da Liberdade, 185
☎ 21 319 89 00
🄵 21 319 89 50
38–42,000esc.
This hotel in a well-renovated 1950s building, is one of the few in the city centre to boast a swimming pool and tennis court. You do pay for the luxury, though.

Altis★★★★
Rua Castilho, 11
☎ 21 314 24 96
🄵 21 354 86 96
28–35,000esc.
This luxury hotel, a stone's throw from Avenida da Liberdade, offers very competitive prices. Don't miss the marvellous view from the panoramic Dom Fernando restaurant on the top floor.

Orion Eden★★★★
Praça dos Restauradores, 24
Metro Restauradores
☎ 21 321 66 00
🄵 21 321 66 66
35–40,000esc.
The Orion hotel residence offers good-quality apartments in the Eden theatre's splendid Art Deco building. With the Tivoli, it's one of the few hotels in the district to have a rooftop swimming pool.

Florida★★★
Av. Duque de Palmela, 32
Metro Pombal
☎ 21 353 46 83
🄵 21 354 35 84
18–20,000esc.
A very functional hotel, practically overlooking Praça Marquês de Pombal. The rooms are good-quality without being luxurious. Good value for money.

Miraparque★★★
Avenida Sidonio Pais, 12
Metro Pombal
☎ 21 352 42 86
🄵 21 357 89 20
18,500–22,000esc.

Some of the rooms here have a marvellous view of the Parque Eduardo VII. Make sure you ask for one when you book, as they're the only thing of interest about this comfortable but unpretentious hotel.

Lisboa Plaza★★★★
Travessa do Salitre, 7
☎ 21 346 39 22
🄵 21 347 16 30
24–30,000esc.
This hotel, belonging to the Best Western chain, has been recently renovated by the Portuguese architect Lucinio Cruz. It offers first-rate, attentive service.

Mundial★★★★
Rua Dom Duarte, 4
Praça Martim Moniz
☎ 21 886 31 01
🄵 21 887 91 29
16–20,000esc.
Like the Praça Martim Moniz itself, this 1950s building has recently been renovated and restored to its former glory. It's a luxury hotel offering pleasant rooms in the very heart of the Baixa.

Lisboa★★★★
Rua Barata Salgueiro, 5A
☎ 21 355 41 31
🄵 21 355 41 39
21–35,000esc.
This slightly impersonal hotel, a few minutes walk from Avenida da Liberdade, offers impeccable service and comfort.

Lisboa Tejo★★★★
(residencial)
Poço do Borratem, 4
☎ 21 886 51 82
18–20,000esc.
This hotel opened in 1994, and combines modern comfort with old-fashioned charm. The adjacent well (poço) has been tastefully restored, and has given the street its name (Poço do Borratem).

Eduardo VII★★★
(residencial)
Av. Fontes Pereira de Melo, 5
☎ 21 353 01 41
🄵 21 353 38 79
10–25,000esc.
This hotel near the Parque Eduardo VII offers excellent value for money, which makes up for its

charmless façade. The Brazilian lunch on Saturday is a must.

Coimbra Madrid★★★
(residencial)
Praça da Figueira, 3
3° and 4°
☎ 21 342 17 60
🖷 21 342 32 64
8–15,000esc.
The main advantage of this fairly basic guest house is its location on Praça da Figueira, which is very lively at night.

Jorge V★★★
(pensão)
Rua Mouzinho
da Silveira, 3
☎ 21 356 25 25
🖷 21 315 03 19
18–28,000esc.
This is a comfortable modern hotel, with well-equipped rooms in a quiet street near Avenida da Liberdade.

Presidente★★
(residencial)
Rua Alexandre
Herculano, 13
☎ 21 353 95 01
🖷 21 352 02 72
18–20,000esc.
A rather impersonal hotel, often frequented by businessmen, offering pleasant rooms and good location.

Suiço-Atlantico★★
(residencial)
Rua da Gloria, 3–19
☎ 21 346 17 13
🖷 21 346 90 13
12–15,000esc.
A popular hotel in a picturesque setting, close to the Elevador da Gloria.

Alegria★★
(residencial)
Praça da Alegria, 12
R/C and 1° D.
☎ 21 322 06 70
🖷 21 347 80 70
8–12,000esc.
Clean, simple rooms overlooking a charming little square close to the city centre.

Dona Maria II★
(pensão)
Rua das Portas de
S. Antão, 9/3
☎ 21 342 52 68
1,500–6,000esc.

This is without a doubt one of the least expensive guest houses in the centre of Lisbon. The rooms are clean but without any frills, and there are communal showers. It's highly recommended if you're on a budget.

Principe Real/ Sao Bento

Bôtanico★★★
(pensão)
Rua da Mãe d'Agua, 16/20
☎ 21 342 03 92
🖷 21 342 01 25
18–20,000esc.
A pleasant hotel which offers good-quality service in a quiet district close to the botanical garden. You'll also be just a step away from the very lively streets of the Bairro Alto.

Principe Real★★★
(pensão)
Rua da Alegria, 53
☎ 21 346 01 16
🖷 21 342 21 04
22–25,000esc.
This is a delightful place to stay, a little way away from Avenida da Liberdade and its busy traffic. The rooms are fairly large considering the district, and the service is friendly.

Bairro Alto

Camões★★
Travessa do Poço
da Cidade, 38; 1° and 2°
☎ 21 346 75 10
🖷 21 346 40 48
5–10,000esc.
This is a good place to stay, ocated in the heart of the Bairro Alto. It offers spacious rooms and a warm welcome, but avoid it if you're looking for peace and quiet in the evening.

Globo★
(pensão)
Rua da Teixeira, 11
☎ 21 346 22 79
4–8,000esc.

This is a pleasant guest house if you're on a budget but want reasonably comfortable surroundings. All the rooms have en-suite bathrooms and it's only two minutes on foot from the Port Wine Institute.

HOTELS

This is one of the hotels that opened for Expo '98. It has a marvellous view of the exhibition site and Ponte de Vasco de Gama, and is easily accessible from the airport.

Further from the centre, in the Avenidas district

Berna★★★
(pensão)
Av. Antonio Serpa, 11–13
☎ 21 793 67 67
☏ 21 793 62 78
12–17,000esc.
If you want to avoid the hustle and bustle of the Baixa, this guest house not far from the Fundação Calouste Gulbenkian and its magnificent park is a pleasant alternative.

Ibis★★
(residencial)
Avenida João Malhoa,
Praça de Espanha
☎ 21 727 31 81
☏ 21 727 38 27
9–11,000esc.
The usual basic comfort of the famous French hotel chain. It's a pity it's a little out of the way.

Alfama/Castelo

Palacio Belmonte★★★★
Pàtio dom Fradique, 14
Castelo
☎ 21 886 25 82
☏ 21 886 25 92
40–50,000esc.
This hotel is the height of luxury. It consists of just a few rooms in the heart of the old castle district that have been restored by the architect Frédéric Coustols. The view from the windows is breathtaking. Some of the scenes in the Wim Wenders film, Lisbon Story, were shot in this magical setting.

S. João das Praças★
Rua S. João das Praças, 97
☎ and ☏ 21 886 25 91
6–10,000esc.
A very well-maintained guest house in an outstanding location at the foot of the cathedral, offering decent rooms and spotless bathrooms.

Parque das Nações

Melia Oriente★★★★
(pensão)
Avenida D. João II
☎ 21 893 00 00
☏ 21 893 00 99
26–30,000esc.

HOTELS

Baixa

Churrasqueria Cafreal*
Rua das Portas de Sto. Antão, 71/73
☎ 21 346 84 47.
The king of frango no churrasqo (chicken on a spit) is well worth a visit during your stay, if only at lunchtime. Simple, tasty and cheap!

Gambrinus***
Rua das Portas de Sto. Antão, 25
☎ 21 342 14 66.
This place is a Lisbon institution for its cellar and fine selection of seafood. It was one of the first restaurants in Portugal to be awarded a Michelin star, but sadly it doesn't quite live up to its reputation at present.

Chiado/Bairro Alto

Cervejaria Trindade**
Rua Nova da Trindade, 20
☎ 21 342 35 06
Every day except Mon. and holidays 9am-2am.
This is a very pleasant place for a brasserie-style lunch or dinner. Choose the first room, lined entirely with blue and yellow azulejos, to tuck into your platter of seafood.

Sul**
Rua do Norte, 13
☎ 21 346 24 49
Every day except Mon. 12.30pm-2am.
A wine bar that doubles as restaurant, where you could easily get carried away. The specialities are based on meat imported directly from Argentina or Brazil and whatever produce looks good in the market that day. Allow around 3,000esc per person.

S. Bento/Santos

Casa do Mexico
Av. D. Carlos I, 40
☎ 21 396 55 00.
The small staircase leading down to the restaurant is narrow and fairly steep, but don't be put off. The vaulted room in the basement is pleasantly decor-ated in the style of a Mexican hacienda. You get tequi-la and guacamole to welcome you, and the fajitas are excellent.

Café dos Santos
Largo de Santos, 15
☎ 21 397 79 12.
A brand-new brasserie with a minimalist, chic decor that's already become very fashionable. Come here for good Portuguese cuisine. The house beef comes with a very wide choice of molhos (sauces). Expect to pay 1,600–2,500esc for a main course.

Armazém F
Rua da Cintura, Armazém, 65
Cais do Gas. Santos
☎ 21 322 01 60.
Another warehouse that's made way for a fashionable bar, restaurant and disco. The decor's fine, but with its neon lights and very loud music, it isn't an intimate setting. Creative, even daring, cuisine.

Bairro Alto

Consenso
Rua Academia das Ciências, 1A
☎ 21 346 86 11.
Four rooms based on the four elements. You can decide for yourself whether you want a cool marine or earthy setting, or a fiery evening. Excellent international cuisine.

Casa Nostra
Travessa do Poço da Cidade, 10
☎ 21 342 59 31.
A fashionable little Italian restaurant where it's essential to book, as there's only room for the fortunate few. The decor is a little cold, but the pasta is good.

Lapa (quartier)

Café da Lapa
Rua São João da Mata, 30
☎ 21 396 26 83
Every day except Mon.
The French chef will satisfy the most delicate palates, and the house duck pâté is particularly delicious. The food is nouvelle cuisine in style, but it's served in generous portions. The smart, retro decor makes a good setting for a candlelit dinner for two or a lively meal with friends. Expect to pay around 6,000esc per person.

A Padaria da Lapa
Rua S. Felix, 33 A
☎ 21 395 03 79.
This is the latest restaurant to open its doors in the district. The dining room is decorated in sunny shades of yellow, ochre and orange, with beautiful bouquets of flowers. They serve good, traditional Portuguese cuisine.

Belém/Ajuda/Parque de Monsanto

Espelho d'Agua
Av. Brasilia
☎ 21 301 73 73.
In summer Espelho d'Agua offers a fine open-air esplanade for an elegant dinner opposite the Tagus and the monument to the age of discovery. You'll need to bring a jumper with you, even in the summer months, as it gets quite chilly outside.

Mercado do Peixe
Est. Casal Pedro Teixeira, Alto da Ajuda
☎ 21 363 69 42.
The Mercado do Peixe is renowned as the best fish restaurant in Lisbon. It's in the middle of the Parque de Monsanto, but is worth coming out of your way for if you're looking for really fresh fish. It's fairly expensive at around 10,000esc per person.

Vela Latina
Doca do Bom Sucesso
☎ 21 301 71 18.
This restaurant, on the banks of the Tagus, resembles a rather smart sailing club. It serves a tasty sea-based cuisine and tends to be full of businessmen at lunchtime.

Docas de Santo Amaro/Alcântara

Speakeasy**
Rocha conde de Obidos, Cais das Oficinas, Armazém, 115
☎ 21 396 42 57.
You can eat well here in a casual decor of brick walls and odd furniture while watching the cargo ships loading and unloading. There's excellent music every evening except Sunday, with jazz, blues and a jam session.

Doca Jardim do Marisco/Santa Apolonia

Bica do Sapato
Avenida Infante D. Henrique
Armazem B, Cais da Pedra
☎ 21 881 03 20
Every day.

This fashionable new restaurant, which opened in June 1999, is a place where you're sure to eat well and be ideally placed to see some of the local celebrities. The owners are all well-known, and one of them, Manuel Reis, has taken charge of the 1970s-style interior decoration. The chef, Joaquim Figueiredo, is one of the best known in the country, so the cuisine is always up to scratch. There's a sushi bar on the first floor, and booking is essential.

Clube dos Empresarios Antonio Clara
Av. da Republica, 38
☎ 21 796 63 80.

This very select restaurant in a magnificent 19th-century residence is frequented by businessmen at lunchtime, and has the atmosphere of an English club in the evening.

Clube VII
Parque Eduardo VII
☎ 21 386 75 52.

The Setimo restaurant in the select Club 'Seven' is well-known to Lisbon society. It's a very pleasant place to have lunch in summer, but dinner is a very formal affair. There is a good view from the terrace down to the park and the courts of the tennis club.

Sintra

Hackrell Café
Praça da Republica, 12/14
Sintra
☎ 21 923 57 10,
21 923 08 96.

One of the trendiest restaurants in Sintra. You can expect to pay 5–6,000esc per person for dinner.

Opera Prima
Rua Consiglieri Pedroso, 2A Sintra
☎ 21 924 45 18.

This place offers a vaulted cellar, ochre walls, an endless beer list and very strong cocktails. It's the meeting-place of the young of the district, with jazz concerts on Thursdays.

RESTAURANTS

BARS, CAFÉS, TEAROOMS AND JAZZ CLUBS

Docas/ Cais do Sodré/ Avenida 24 de Julho

Art'z
Armazém 113,
Rocha Conde de Obidos
Doca de Santo Amaro
Every day except Mon.
8pm-4am.
This, the latest of the dockland nightspots, has serious ambitions. It's successful in being both an avant-garde art gallery and an original and unusual place to spend the evening. The paintings on show are interesting and the clientele is essentially made up from the art and fashion worlds. You can also have dinner with an uninterrupted view of the port thanks to the restaurant on the first floor.

Hennessy's
Rua do Cais do Sodré,
32/38
☎ 21 343 10 64
Every day 10.30-11am,
2pm-2am (Fri. and Sat.
4am).
Everything has been preserved in this former shop, which belonged to an Irish tailor in the early 20th century – the panelling, sewing machines, fabrics and reels of thread. The Guinness flows freely, and after 10.30pm the conversation gives way to music.

Bairro Alto

Artis
Rua do Diário de
Notícias, 95
☎ 21 342 47 95.
Come here if you want to get away from high-tech decor and you'll find a cosy place to spend the evening in the midst of a varied and broad-minded crowd.

Bar Nova
Rua da Rosa, 261
☎ 21 346 28 34.
The most famous 'salad and sushi bar' in the Bairro Alto has lost a little of its shine recently, but is still worth visiting.

Snob
Rua do Século 178
☎ 21 346 37 23.
One of the trendiest bars in the district, where you're vetted at the weekend.

S. Bento

Xico's Bar
Rua Correia Garção, 3
☎ 21 390 10 22.
An ideal place to have a drink opposite the Parliament building before tackling the climb of Rua S. Bento and doing the rounds of the district's antique dealers. It's an inspired choice, since it also houses exhibitions of paintings and sculptures.

Lapa

El Salseiro Lapa
Rua de Buenos Aires, 31B
☎ 21 396 80 17
Open Mon.-Sat. until
2am.
Latin America in the heart of Lapa – delicious tropical drinks and Mexican nibbles make this a great venue. The music is 'a vontade' (as much as you like), including salsa and rumba.

Chiado

Casa Havaneza
Largo do Chiado, 25
☎ 21 342 03 40
Closed Sun.
This shop in the Chiado has been a must for cigar lovers since 1864. Connoisseurs will find their favourite Butz-Choquins, Castellos and Dunhills here, and it's just opened an area reserved exclusively for Havana smokers.

Cascais

Mise en Scène
Rua Luiz Xavier
Palmeirim, 12
☎ and 🖷 21 484 23 13
Every day 11am-8pm,
closed Mon.
This is a very unusual tea room. It's been tastefully decorated by a French couple, and there are floral arrangements and designer clothes to buy, in addition to decorative objects. More than anything, it's a nice place to have lunch, thanks to the delicious selection of breads, generous duck salads and wide selection of teas.

Bairro Alto

Adega Machado
Rua do Norte 91
☎ 21 342 87 13.
A 1930s fado house that's still run by the Machado family. It's a pity such a charming place is also frequented by tour groups. It's essential to book in advance.

Café Luso
Tv. da Queimada, 10
☎ 21 342 22 81.
This is the legendary place where the famous singer, Amália Rodrigues, made her debut in the pre-war years. Very reasonable prices for an atmospheric dinner and show (3,500esc per person).

BARS/CAFÉS

FOR NATURE LOVERS

The estuaries of the Tagus and the Sado (its main tributary in the south) are renowned for their flora and fauna, and recently became highly-protected nature reserves. A trip up the Tagus estuary is an unique opportunity to see hundreds of birds that are very rare in Europe, such as the white stilt and little tern. Jeep tours run by Safari Samora Correia (☎ 063/62034 or 0931/603459), cost 10,000esc per person per day, including meals and a visit to a bull-breeding farm. Another excursion you really shouldn't miss is a visit to Rio Sado to observe the dolphin colony. You leave Setúbal on board a motorboat or sailing boat for a day devoted to the observation of one of the largest families of dolphins still living in Europe, which numbers around 40 adults. To arrange a trip, contact Vie Sauvage, Rua Antonio Pedro, 125/A, 1000 Lisboa, ☎ 21 357 22 19, 🖷 21 314 07 09, e-mail: natureza@esoterica.pt, 7,500esc per person, including lunch.

A WALK IN THE SERRA DE SINTRA

If you're staying a little longer in Lisbon, the Serra de Sintra, which is around 30km/19 miles away, is also worth visiting for the day. Leaving from the city centre by car, several routes are possible. You can go via the Castelo dos Mouros, an 8th-century fortress built by the Moors that dominates the town, or via the Convento dos Capuchos, a hermitage where you can spend a few moments in silence. All the routes wind their way through the imposing eucalyptus and coniferous forest and also allow you to see the abundant vegetation of the Serra and the roofs of a number of aristocratic villas dating from the 19th century. Some of these have now been restored and are open to the public. For further information contact the Sintra Tourist Information Office, Praça da República, ☎ 21 923 11 57, 🖷 21 923 51 76. The best beaches in the vicinity of Lisbon are on the Costa da Caparica. Around twenty beaches succeed each other along this 19km/12 mile strip of sand between Caparica and Cabo Espichel. As soon as the weather turns fine, crowds of city-dwellers rush here to sunbathe on Sundays. The beaches are easy to get to from Lisbon and are only 20 minutes from the city (not counting the traffic jams) by car or bus (no. 53 from Praça d'Espanha). You can also go by ferry to Calcalhas, then take any bus. In Caparica, a picturesque little train runs along the coast linking the various beaches.

FOR ARMCHAIR TRAVELLERS

If you're feeling lazy and want to spend the rest of your stay sunbathing beside the swimming pool of your hotel, here are some books that will allow you to make your way round Lisbon without leaving the comfort of your deck chair:

The History of the Siege of Lisbon by José Saramango

Declares Pereira and *Requiem: A Hallucination* by Antonio Tabucchi

The Book of Disquiet and *Lisbon: What a Tourist Should See* by Fernando Pessoa

The Following Story by Cees Nooteboom

PRACTICALITIES

NOTES

routard

Titles for 2000:

Ireland	1 84202 024 2
Paris	1 84202 027 7

Coming in 2001:

Andalucia & Southern Spain	1 84202 028 5
Belgium	1 84202 022 6
Brittany	1 84202 020 X
California, Nevada & Arizona	1 84202 025 0
Cuba	1 84202 062 5
Egypt	1 84202 137 0
Greek Islands & Athens	1 84202 023 4
Mexico	1 84202 138 9
Pas de Calais	1 84202 139 7
Provence & the Côte d'Azur	1 84202 019 6
Rome & Southern Italy	1 84202 021 8
Southern India & Sri Lanka	1 84202 140 0
Thailand	1 84202 029 3
West Canada & Ontario	1 84202 031 5

Titles in this series are available through all good
booksellers, or can be ordered by calling
01903 828800, quoting ref. RT3 (in the UK).

HACHETTE VACANCES

A unique series of regional guides in colour that focus on the needs of families and those in search of an active holiday. Packed with hundreds of suggestions for places to visit, sights to see and things to do – as well as providing detailed information about the region's culture, heritage and history. To help you get even more out of your holiday, a selection of discount vouchers is also included.

Titles currently published:

Brittany	1 84202 007 2
Languedoc-Roussillon	1 84202 008 0
Poitou-Charentes	1 84202 009 9
Provence & The Côte d'Azur	1 84202 006 4
Pyrenees & Gascony	1 84202 015 3
South West France	1 84202 014 5

Forthcoming titles:

Catalonia	1 84202 099 4
Corsica	1 84202 100 1
Normandy	1 84202 097 8
Perigord & Dordogne	1 84202 098 6

Titles are available through all good booksellers, or by calling 01903 828800, quoting ref. RT1 (in the UK).

HACHETTE

Make the most of your mini-break

Great Weekend titles provide all the information you need to ensure that you really get to know a city in just a few days — from advice on what to see, where to stay and where to eat out, to exploring the city's character through its culture and lifestyle. Plus a detailed section on where to do your shopping. Full colour throughout and great value for money.

A GREAT WEEKEND *in* ....

AMSTERDAM	1 84202 002 1
BARCELONA	1 84202 005 6
BERLIN	1 84202 061 7
BRUSSELS	1 84202 017 X
FLORENCE	1 84202 010 2
LISBON	1 84202 011 0
LONDON	1 84202 013 7
MADRID	1 84202 095 1
NAPLES	1 84202 016 1
NEW YORK	1 84202 004 8
PARIS	1 84202 001 3
PRAGUE	1 84202 000 5
ROME	1 84202 003 X
VENICE	1 84202 018 8
VIENNA	1 84202 026 9

Forthcoming titles:

DUBLIN	1 84202 096 X

Titles are available through all good booksellers, or by calling 01903 828800, quoting ref. RT2 (in the UK).

HACHETTE